Bed & Breakfast Homes Directory

Homes Away From Home

West Coast

4th Edition

4th Edition

Bed & Breakfast Homes Directory

Homes Away From Home

West Coast

by
Diane Knight

Graphics by Kevin McElvain
Editing by Suzy Blackaby

Library of Congress Catalog Card Number: 85-081398

ISBN 0-942902-03-3

Typography by Jean Graphics, San Jose, California

Printed in the United States of America

Pictured on cover: Cedarym, A Colonial Bed & Breakfast, Redmond, Washington

 KNIGHTTIME PUBLICATIONS

P.O. Box 591
Cupertino, CA 95015

CONTENTS

INTRODUCTION

Here, dear readers, is the fourth edition of *BED & BREAKFAST HOMES DIRECTORY*. To those of you who have followed its development over the years, I am deeply grateful. You obviously know that *B&BHD* takes an approach that is unique in the world of B&B guidebooks. The feedback I get from you is most helpful, and I particularly appreciate it when you recommend *B&BHD* to your friends and to booksellers. Being an independent publisher has many advantages, but gaining wide recognition isn't one of them. Your support is vital.

To new readers, *BED & BREAKFAST HOMES DIRECTORY* is your invitation to take part in our "hospitality network"—a group of hosts dedicated to making your travels along the West Coast the most rewarding possible. I continue to encourage readers to remain open to new experiences. Try an excursion to a place you've never heard of; some of my most memorable trips have taken me far from the beaten path. This book is for travelers (as opposed to tourists), people who want to see more than the places everyone knows about. The true adventurer savors the joy of *discovery*.

I urge you to read the introductory pages in this book, for some of the questions I am asked the most frequently are answered here. Among other things, you will notice that hosts in *BED & BREAKFAST HOMES DIRECTORY* have agreed to honor published rates for our readers at least until the end of 1986. Be sure to mention that you found their B&B in this book and that you have the current edition. You must also have the book to obtain the discounts given to our readers.

A new edition of *BED & BREAKFAST HOMES DIRECTORY* is planned for early 1988. Due to budgetary constraints, supplements will no longer be published. As you may know, conditions at in-home B&Bs are likely to change more frequently than at B&B inns. It is my custom to monitor these changes as nearly as possible. A computer printout of updated information will be available between editions. Readers may request an update at any time; please furnish a stamped, self-addressed, legal-sized envelope.

Knighttime Publications is taking on two additional functions beginning in 1986. First, I have put together a small but very special collection of reading matter (guidebooks and newsletters) that will be available to our readers by mailorder. These particular items, mostly of regional interest, are not widely distributed in chain bookstores. However, they have proven extremely valuable to me in my travels, as well as in learning about the various facets of the bed and breakfast movement.

In addition to *The Knighttime Collection*, we will be publishing a newsletter every two months. It is intended to be a companion to *BED & BREAKFAST HOMES DIRECTORY* by furnishing firsthand information gleaned during my years of traveling to visit host homes. Having by now accumulated a wealth of insights and tips, I welcome the opportunity to share them with readers of *B&BHD*. *The Knighttime Companion* will be inexpensive and simple in format, but packed with information that will enhance your travels to the destinations covered in the book.

Instructions for obtaining the newsletter, the collection of reading materials, and additional copies of *BED & BREAKFAST HOMES DIRECTORY* can be found on page 231.

Finally, I must address the fact that there are glaring omissions of B&B homes in certain areas that *B&BHD* covers, most notably the Monterey Peninsula. Local regulations there strictly forbid lodgings other than commercial establishments—motels, hotels, and inns. Because the area is so appealing and popular, certainly many readers still rank it high on their list of favored destinations. As a service to those who seek the best possible value in lodging, dining, etc., the premier issue of *The Knighttime Companion* (January/February 1986) will carry the feature article, "Best Values on the Monterey Peninsula." Other articles will follow about getting the most for your travel dollar, particularly in areas where prices are notoriously high.

May this edition of *BED & BREAKFAST HOMES DIRECTORY* spark some new discoveries for you.

Diane Knight

The traveler was active; he went strenuously in search of people, of adventure, of experience. The tourist is passive; he expects interesting things to happen to him. He goes "sightseeing."

—Daniel J. Boorstin

ABOUT BED & BREAKFAST IN PRIVATE HOMES

The B&B homes in this directory, in most cases, are strictly private homes, not commercial establishments. As a guest, remember to act with the same courtesy and consideration that you would expect of a guest in your own home.

Most B&BHD hosts aren't innkeepers. They're not in business full time; there may be occasions when hosts can't accommodate you because they'll be on vacation, or because Great-Aunt Martha from Omaha will be using the guest room.

For the most part, there is no daily maid service or room service. Thus, guests should make their own beds and get their own ice (after asking, of course).

With some exceptions, B&B hosts will accept only cash or traveler's checks as payment for accommodations. Be sure to establish the method of payment with your host *before* your visit.

When reserving accommodations in B&B homes, it is very important to agree upon your time of arrival with the host. This is only courteous when you consider that hosts have their own private lives and family obligations. They would like to know when to be at home to greet you. Of course, there's always some flexibility, but arrival time should be discussed. If it appears you will be later than planned, a phone call would be appreciated.

Room rates include at least a Continental breakfast. In some cases, the rate includes a full breakfast; in others, there may be an extra charge if you wish a full breakfast. This is considered a complimentary meal.

Many hosts look forward to having guests join them for a family-style breakfast. In certain situations, if the guest unit is totally separate and has cooking facilities, the host will simply leave the ingredients for breakfast so that guests can prepare it for themselves. There are hosts who will be glad to serve you breakfast in your room, or even in bed. As in many phases of B&B travel, the accent is on *variety*.

HOW TO USE THIS DIRECTORY

For each listing:

The first line tells either the name of the host or the name given to the B&B home and the phone number to call for reservations.

The second line gives the mailing address of the home to use if you're writing for reservations.

The third line, in parentheses, indicates the general location of the home. You should get specific directions from your host.

Next you'll find a descriptive paragraph about the B&B home. It often tells something about the unique qualities of the home itself, the setting, the host, points of interest in the area.

The second paragraph indicates whether there are indoor pets and gives the host's preferences, such as "no smoking" or "children welcome." These appear in a consistent sequence in each listing. They are given only if the host has indicated a specific policy on the subject. The paragraph also lists facilities or features available to guests, such as "laundry" or "hot tub."

Available transportation is sometimes indicated, as well as the host's willingness to pick up guests at a nearby airport (mainly for the benefit of private pilots).

The following code refers to the heading at the end of each description:

ROOM	Refers to guest unit. The unit may be a room in the host's home, an adjoining apartment, or a separate cottage near the home. Each letter (*A, B,...*) designates one guest unit, whether it has one, two, or more rooms.
BED	Number and type(s) of bed(s) given for each guest unit. This means total beds per unit. **T** = twin, **D** = double, **Q** = queen, **K** = king.
BATH	**Shd** means you'll share a bath with the host. **Shd*** means the bath is shared by other guests, if present. (Chances are you may have it all to yourself.) **Pvt** means the bath goes with the guest unit and is not shared by the host. It may be down the hall, but it is all yours.
ENTRANCE	**Main** indicates you'll use the main entrance of the home. **Sep** means there's a separate entrance for guests.
FLOOR	Floor of each guest room is indicated by number in most cases. **LL** indicates lower level, with steps down. **1G** means a ground level room.
DAILY RATES	**S** refers to a single (one person); **D** refers to a double (two persons); **EP** refers to the rate charged for each extra person (above two) traveling with your party. **Some of the rates quoted include a local tax; others will have tax added.**

Example:

Room	Bed	Bath	Entrance	Floor	Daily Rates S - D (EP)
A	1K	Pvt	Main	2	$30 - $36 ($6)

Room (or unit) A has one king-sized bed, a private bath, uses the main entrance to the home, is on the second floor. One person will pay $30; two persons will pay $36; each extra person will pay $6.

AC = Air Conditioning; **VCR** = Video Cassette Recorder; **AARP** = American Association of Retired Persons; **BART** = Bay Area Rapid Transit (in San Francisco Bay Area).

HOW TO ARRANGE A B&B VISIT

1. ● Try to plan your visit as far ahead as possible. This helps to ensure you'll get to stay in the B&B home of your choice. Notify your host immediately of any change in plans.

2. ● Call your host for reservations before 9 p.m. Be sure to allow for the time difference if you're not on Pacific Time.

3. ● Carefully check details about the listing you're considering before calling or writing. Confirm with your host anything that's not clear to you. Ask pertinent questions!

4. ● Check what form(s) of payment your host will accept. Ask if a deposit is required.

5. ● Agree on time of arrival.

Hosts listed in BED & BREAKFAST HOMES DIRECTORY have agreed to honor rates stated in the directory until the end of 1986.

The information contained in these listings has been prepared with great care, but we cannot guarantee that it is complete or in all cases correct. It is the user's responsibility to verify important information when making arrangements.

North
Coast

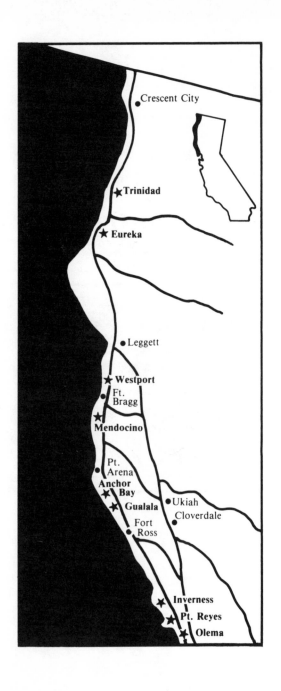

Waves, woodlands, and wind-wafted fog work to enchant the traveler to the North Coast—the spell of nature is irresistible. From the surf-swept shores of the Sonoma and Mendocino coastlines to the towering trees of the Redwood Highway, the scenery is a frontier for the exploring imagination.

The contrast of wood and wave is perhaps nowhere more dramatic than at Point Reyes National Seashore. The steep cliffs, sighted four hundred years ago by Sir Francis Drake, guard a peninsula of dense forest, fern-filled canyons, and open pasture land. Beach aficionados can choose between expansive sandy strands and futuristic convolutions of rock. Tule elk, deer, sea lions, huge jack rabbits, and three hundred sixty-one species of birds share the space with you; migrating whales cruise by each winter.

From Bodega Bay north to Gualala, rolling hills spill into the sea, where white foam swirls around imposing sea stacks. Here too, Fort Ross—historic survivor of the nineteenth-century Russian presence in California—sits high and dry on an isolated bluff. You can climb the stairs of the restored stockade to watch the waves of the past wash up below.

"Talk to me of Mendocino" sings the song, and indeed, nostalgia has been known to overtake even the least sentimental in this transposed bit of old New England. The town itself has sunk its sturdy roots into a precarious-looking headland jutting into the sea and studiously ignores the insistent pounding of the surf at its door. The nucleus of a coastal community of artists and artisans, Mendocino offers an abundance of galleries and shops housed in nineteenth-century buildings.

Seasoned wave-watchers recommend Mendocino Headlands State Park for a show-stopping performance of water in motion, while from Fort Bragg, wilderness devotees ride the "Skunks" (railway cars originally named for their pungent gas engines) through forty miles of redwood groves inaccessible by car.

A compelling symbol of California, the legendary redwoods rise in original splendor along the Redwood Highway that stretches from Leggett to Crescent City. It is hard not to think of these trees as the stuff of myth. The hushed messages of their branches tell a story of enduring grandeur. They are a discovery that never ages, and travelers reaching the town of Eureka—meaning "I found it!"—can only add, "You can't miss it."

Ed & Arlene Aaron   **(707) 884-3790**
P.O. Box 130, Gualala, CA 95445
(35001 Woodside Court, Anchor Bay)

The Aarons' redwood home is in perfect harmony with its surroundings. The forested setting allows great ocean views from most of the rooms. The living area has a fireplace, comfortable seating, and some beautiful work by local artists. It's just the place for relaxed conversation with the Aarons, people who truly enjoy having visitors. Ed, a retired veterinarian, will be glad to show you the exotic plants he raises. Arlene's special interests include Oriental cooking, tennis, fishing, and her pets. The private guest suite has its own bath, deck, and, of course, the view.

Dog and two cats in residence; no pets or children; full breakfast; TV; deck; soaking tub available in hosts' bathroom; good hiking nearby; some French spoken; airport pickup (Ocean Ridge). 10% discount to seniors.

Room	Bed	Bath	Entrance	Floor	Daily Rates S - D	(EP)
A	2T	Pvt	Main	1	$45-$50	

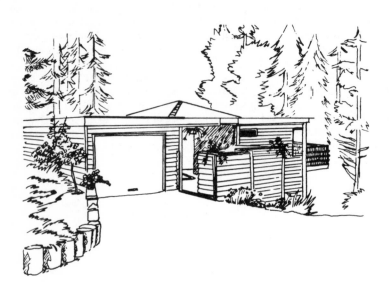

Old Town Bed & Breakfast (707) 445-3951
1521 Third Street, Eureka, CA 95501
(Third near P; north end of Old Town district)

This historic home was built in 1871, and was bought by lumber magnate William Carson in 1872. He lived in it until 1915, when it was sold and moved to its present location. More recently, the whole house has been refurbished. Each room is carefully decorated to allow guests a nostalgic glimpse into Eureka's past. Lovely antiques fill rooms with intriguing names: Tulips & Evergreen, Raspberry Parfait, Blue Calico, Samoa, and English Ivy. William Carson's celebrated Victorian mansion is located nearby; you may wish to walk or bicycle by it on your way to explore Old Town's architecture, shops, and restaurants. At the end of the day, hosts Floyd and Carolyn Hall invite you to relax in the Raspberry Parlor with wine and hors d'oeuvres. They want to make your stay in Eureka a warm and memorable experience.

No pets; no children under twelve; full breakfast; afternoon refreshments; bicycles; bus transportation; airport pickup (Eureka-Arcata). 10% discount for five days or longer.

Room	Bed	Bath	Entrance	Floor	Daily Rates S - D	(EP)
A	2T or 1K	Pvt	Main	2	$45-$55	
B	1Q	Shd*	Main	2	$40-$50	
C	1Q	Shd*	Main	2	$40-$50	
D	1D	Pvt	Main	2	$35-$45	
E	1Q	Pvt	Main	1	$45-$55	

The Stevens House

(707) 445-9080

917 Third Street, Eureka, CA 95501
(Between J and K; north end of Old Town district)

Carter and Company, who brought us the incredible Victorian reproduction, Carter House Inn, has struck again, this time with an original Victorian just down the street. Debbie Pizzuto hosts The Stevens House and keeps the standards of hospitality high. She serves delicious Continental breakfasts, helps guests with dinner plans, and offers tips on the area. White walls throughout the house show off the colorful work of local artists. Oriental rugs and bright bedcoverings add lively touches to the decor. My favorite feature is the stunning collection of antique pine furniture from England. Distinctive style and good taste prevail at The Stevens House—just what we've come to expect from the Carters.

No pets; bus transportation; airport pickup (Eureka-Arcata). On weeknights, a room with private bath can be arranged at $10 extra. Carter House Inn, at 1033 Third Street, has seven rooms available with full breakfast. Rates range from $60 to $125. Phone (707) 445-1390 for reservations.

Room	Bed	Bath	Entrance	Floor	Daily Rates S - D	(EP)
A	1Q	Shd*	Main	2	$55	
B	1Q	Shd*	Main	2	$55	
C	1Q	Shd*	Main	2	$55	
D	1Q	Shd*	Main	2	$55	

The Iseman Residence

(707) 884-3584

P.O. Box 888, Gualala, CA 95445
(West of Highway 1, one mile north of town)

I find Gualala appealing for a number of reasons: it isn't too touristy; there's just enough to see and do on a weekend; it feels more remote than it really is; the people have a keen sense of community; and the coastline is just beginning to get that rugged look of the north coast. At The Iseman Residence, you'll have a private apartment that's connected to the house by an atrium. It has a living room with a wonderful ocean view, a wet bar, a bedroom, and a bath. The Isemans' cultural interests include collecting the work of their favorite artists, many of whom are local, which appears throughout the house. The pleasant environment may tempt you to simply curl up with a good book, but exploring the rocky coast is enticing, too. The natural beauty and salty fresh air could be just the elixir you need.

No pets; TV; phone; sofa bed in living room; shops, galleries, and two fine restaurants, plus golf, tennis, canoeing, hiking, and beachcombing nearby; Italian spoken; airport pickup (Ocean Ridge, Sea Ranch). Weekly rates available.

Room	Bed	Bath	Entrance	Floor	Daily Rates S - D	(EP)
A	2T or 1K	Pvt	Sep	1	$65-$75	($10)

Susan Brayton & Elizabeth Campbell   **(415) 669-7218**
P.O. Box 644, Inverness, CA 94937
(105 Vision Road, west of Sir Francis Drake at Yacht Club)

Susan and Elizabeth's home is the sort of place where friends like to gather. The living room is highlighted by wood-paneled walls, a large brick fireplace, floors covered with colorful rugs from Afghanistan, and sofas made for comfort and conversation. The natural, unhurried atmosphere reflects the general feeling of the Inverness-Point Reyes area. For B&B guests, a simply furnished bedroom with private bath is quiet and relaxing. People who visit are usually ready for a good rest after hiking on park trails, exploring the seashore, and checking out oyster farms and local crafts. The casual friendliness of this B&B home makes it a welcome retreat.

Cat in residence; no smoking. EP rate is for child over four; room not suitable for three adults.

Room	Bed	Bath	Entrance	Floor	Daily Rates S - D	(EP)
A	1D	Shd	Main	1G	$35-$40	($10)

MacLean House
(415) 669-7392
or 837-4434

P.O. Box 651, Inverness, CA 94937
(One block above town of Inverness and Tomales Bay)

What could be a more perfect setting than Inverness for the perfect Scottish guest house? Among trees overlooking Tomales Bay is the redwood-shingled home of Ginny and Bob Cuenin. It has been renovated and furnished with great attention to detail, carrying out the Scottish theme through the main quarters and the guest rooms below. The clan MacLean tartan provides the color scheme, looking crisp and clean against the white walls of each spacious room. Lovely antiques and brass accents complete the picture, adding up to the utmost in quality lodgings. Flowers and birds abound in this quiet, often sunny location. Point Reyes National Seashore and some excellent local restaurants have always been good reasons to visit the area; now the Cuenins and MacLean House are also high on *my* list.

No pets or RV parking; smoking in rooms discouraged; private patio.

Room	Bed	Bath	Entrance	Floor	Daily Rates S - D	(EP)
A	1T & 1D	Pvt	Sep	1	$60	($10)
B	2D	Pvt	Sep	1	$60	($10)

Mendocino Tennis Club & Lodge   **(707) 937-0007**
43250 Little Lake Road, Mendocino, CA 95460
(Two miles east of Mendocino village)

It's mostly sunny in the redwoods and pines where the Mendocino Tennis Club & Lodge was built. There's a barbecue area, three tennis courts, a swimming pool, and a spa for members and overnight guests. Accommodations include three bedrooms with private baths, a lounging area, and a kitchen. You prepare breakfast at your own convenience; ingredients are provided. The rustic lodge-type building has an informal atmosphere and quiet surroundings, making it an ideal escape for those who enjoy playing tennis *and* exploring the Mendocino coast.

No pets; children welcome; kitchen; swimming pool and spa. (B&B guests have exclusive use after 5:00 p.m.); tennis courts; Room C has deck and rollaway bed; A has attached bath. Brochure available.

Room	Bed	Bath	Entrance	Floor	Daily Rates S - D	(EP)
A	1Q	Pvt	Main	1	$60	
B	1Q	Pvt	Main	2	$55	
C	1Q	Pvt	Main	2	$60	($10)

Pelican Inn - Westport
707/964 5588

The Wool Loft   **(707) 937-0377**
32751 Navarro Ridge Road, Albion, CA 95410
(Ten miles south of Mendocino)

The Wool Loft's setting overlooking the sea reminds me of some B&Bs in Ireland or Scotland. Sheep graze in nearby fields; the family garden and henhouse contribute food to the table. Jan and Sid offer three cheery guest rooms with private baths in the main house to guests who prefer traditional B&B treatment. The Wool Loft itself is a separate accommodation (D). It's a spacious studio apartment with queen-sized bed, fully equipped kitchen, bath, wood-burning stove, and huge windows with stunning river and ocean views. Quiet and cozy seclusion on the famous Mendocino coast is yours if you choose The Wool Loft.

Dogs and cat in residence; no pets, children, or smoking; gather eggs for breakfast if desired; deck and fireplace in main house; firewood provided in Wool Loft; Room C has river and ocean view. Brochure available. Seventh day free for weekly stays.

Room	Bed	Bath	Entrance	Floor	Daily Rates S - D	(EP)
A	1Q	Pvt	Main	1	$50	
B	2T	Pvt	Main	1	$50	
C	1Q	Pvt	Main	1	$60	
D	1Q	Pvt	Sep	2	$75	

PB 60
continental breakfast Queen
45

21

Bear Valley Bed & Breakfast   **(415) 663-1777**
Box 33, Olema, CA 94950
(88 Bear Valley Road, just off Highway 1)

Ron and JoAnne Nowell offer very homey accommodations in their classic two-story ranch house, circa 1900. The interior has the warmth and informality of old-time country living. An overstuffed sofa and chairs in the living room are perfect for relaxed conversation by the fire's glow. Lace curtains, family quilts, and collected antiques blend beautifully with the colorful weaving by local artists, creating a look throughout the house that is fresh and pleasing. Bear Valley B&B is well located for exploring Point Reyes National Seashore. The new visitors' center and main trailhead are an easy half-mile walk from the front door. Nature lovers are ecstatic over the richness of the area. There are over two hundred miles of hiking, horseback riding, and bicycling trails, wide open beaches, and birdwatching sites aplenty. The Nowells invite you to come and enjoy the paradise that surrounds them.

No pets, children, or smoking; horse and bicycle rentals nearby. Brochure available. 10% discount for three consecutive days.

Room	Bed	Bath	Entrance	Floor	Daily Rates S - D	(EP)
A	1D	Shd*	Main	2	$55-$60	
B	1D	Shd*	Main	2	$55-$60	
C	2T	Shd*	Main	2	$55-$60	

Jasmine Cottage (415) 663-1166
P.O. Box 56, Point Reyes Station, CA 94956
(Two blocks from town)

If you like being on your own in total peace and seclusion, Jasmine Cottage could be the hideaway you've been looking for. It is the guest cottage for the original Point Reyes Schoolhouse, built in 1879. Karen Gray lives in the masterfully renovated schoolhouse. She has done a remarkable job with the cottage, too. It opens onto a pasture with a beautiful view of Inverness Ridge and backs onto an herb and flower garden. There is a private drive for guests. The interior is a perfect blend of modern efficiency, family antiques, and local artwork. I particularly like the queen-sized bed alcove. There is a fully equipped kitchen, bath, living area with woodburning stove, patio, garden room, and plenty of windows. A desk holds a collection of naturalists' writings and guides to the Point Reyes area. Jasmine Cottage can be what you want it to be—romantic haven, family vacation spot, nature lover's retreat. It is a place to make some dreams come true.

Children welcome; crib available; adjacent to Point Reyes National Seashore and Tomales Bay State Park. Weekly rate is $395. **KNIGHTTIME PUBLICATIONS SPECIAL RATE: $60 Sunday-Thursday nights with this book.

Room	Bed	Bath	Entrance	Floor	Daily Rates	
					S - D	(EP)
A	2T & 1Q	Pvt	Sep	1G	$85	($10)

39 Cypress   **(415) 663-1709**
P.O. Box 176, Point Reyes Station, CA 94956
(Near Point Reyes National Seashore)

Julia Bartlett feels a special connection to the Point Reyes area and, in particular, to the spot where she's made her home. One easily understands this after being a guest at 39 Cypress. The passive solar house is nestled into a hillside and faces a pastoral scene where cattle graze and all seems right with the world. Inside, there's a strong feeling of "home"—a cozy fireplace, floors covered with aging Oriental rugs, warm quilts to sleep under. The house is natural and rustic, with an ambiance of warmth and comfort. Throughout the house, original works of art catch the eye. There are skylights in every room, and from your bed at night, you may see stars and hear the hooting of owls. In the morning, you might awaken to the sound of gentle horses munching on the greenery just outside the house. Julia can provide a wealth of information for guests about the Point Reyes-Inverness area.

Two cats in residence; no pets or children; TV; patio. Midweek rates are $5 less.

Room	Bed	Bath	Entrance	Floor	Daily Rates S - D	(EP)
A	1D	Shd	Main	1G	$55-$60	
B	1D	Shd	Main	1G	$55-$60	
C	1T	Shd	Main	1G	$55	

Trinidad Bed & Breakfast   **(707) 677-0840**
560 Edwards Street, P.O. Box AU, Trinidad, CA 95570
(Twenty-two miles north of Eureka, just west of U.S. 101)

Discovering Trinidad for the first time is thrilling enough, but I was overjoyed to find the perfect place to stay while doing it. It's been said that Trinidad is the north coast's best kept secret. Well, it won't be for long. Hosts Carol Kirk and Heidi Atwood have an ideal location overlooking Trinidad Bay, with the lighthouse directly across the street. The lovely Cape Cod home has been newly renovated for B&B guests. There are three charming, country-style rooms, each with a spectacular view of the coastline and harbor. Outdoor buffs will love the myriad activities close by. A number of beaches, parks, and trails await the beachcomber, hiker, photographer, and angler. An easily accessible trail around Trinidad Head leads to great spots for picnicking or watching whales and sea lions. You can even walk to dinner, an advantage to those who appreciate a footloose vacation. Explore Trinidad with someone special. It's that kind of place.

No pets or small children; smoking on balcony or porch; common room; airport pickup (Eureka-Arcata). Brochure available. Ask about winter rates. ****KNIGHTTIME PUBLICATIONS SPECIAL RATE:** 15% discount Sunday-Thursday nights September 15-May 15 with this book.

Room	Bed	Bath	Entrance	Floor	Daily Rates S - D	(EP)
A	1Q	Shd*	Main	2	$60-$65	
B	1Q	Shd*	Main	2	$60-$65	($5)
C	1Q	Pvt	Sep	2	$80-$85	($5)

Howard Creek Ranch (707) 964-6725
P.O. Box 121, Westport, CA 95488 (Keep trying!)
(Three miles north of Westport on Highway 1)

Sally and Sunny invite you to retreat to the romance of yesteryear at Howard Creek Ranch. Their ranch house was built in 1872 by Alfred Howard, newly arrived from the coast of Maine. At one time a stagecoach stop, it is now a quaint and cozy home filled with collectibles and antiques. The guest suites allow privacy, and the old fireplace inspires conversation and fun. The house is set in a wide, secluded valley at the mouth of Howard Creek. It faces the ocean and a wide, sandy beach where you can walk for miles at low tide. At this bed and breakfast resort, you can find your own pace and tune in to the natural beauty all around you.

Dog and two cats in residence; full ranch breakfast; kitchen privileges by arrangement; extra beds available; decks; barbecue; swimming pool; wood-heated hot tub; sauna; massage by reservation. All guest units have sinks; A has a balcony; C has a loft; all except B have skylights. Unit D is a boathouse; E is a cabin; both have woodstoves and electricity. Lower rates off-season and midweek.

Room	Bed	Bath	Entrance	Floor	Daily Rates S - D	(EP)
A	1D & 1Q	Shd	Sep	2	$65	($10)
B	1D & 1K	Shd	Sep	1	$55	($10)
C	1T & 1Q	Shd	Main	2	$50	($10)
D	1D	Shd	Sep	1	$45	
E	1D	Shd	Sep	1	$35	

Central
Coast

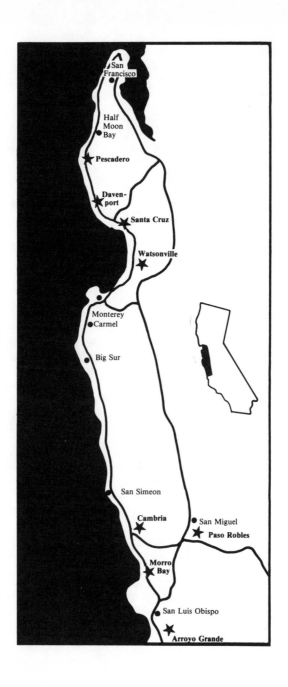

"The Coastside," as the area surrounding Half Moon Bay is known, remains a part of the Pacific's edge where travelers can still make their own discoveries. A favorite country cafe tucked back in the farmlands, a pebble beach where you can still find jade, a redwood grove that stands as a memorial to the dedicated environmentalists who fought for it (the lumber company slashes still visible on the venerable giants marked for cutting) are some of the little-known treasures of the area. The Año Nuevo State Reserve, the James Fitzgerald Marine Reserve, and the Pescadero Wildlife Refuge provide sanctuary for the abundance of coastal wildlife that is yours for the watching, while several state and county parks offer hideaways in the redwoods. A respite from bustling tourism, this stretch of coast allows time and tide their ebb and flow.

Monterey Bay, with its crescent of sandy beaches from Santa Cruz to Carmel, is the heartland of the Central Coast. Here beach-lovers sun, surf, and even swim in the quieter waters of the bay. On the northern shore of the bay, Santa Cruz enjoys a unique ambiance, a mixture of the spontaneous street fun concocted by musicians, dancers, and impromptu actors along the Pacific Garden Mall, the lazy sea lions snoozing beneath the feet of anglers on the municipal pier, and the staid Victorians that keep an eye on the goings-on.

Monterey, on the southern shore, offers a different mood entirely, one steeped in California history and natural beauty. The adobe buildings on the city's Path of History mark its nineteenth-century prominence, while Cannery Row, no longer Steinbeck's turbulent cauldron of the sardine industry, survives as a complex of shops and restaurants. The adjoining town of Pacific Grove has many visitors, some of whom fly in on velvet orange-and-black wings. The Monarch butterflies hang out in select groves of pines from October to March. Carmel-by-the-Sea, a few miles south, is still trying to be a quaint little village in the forest, but its bumper crop of shops, galleries, and restaurants gives it an air of sophistication.

For some people, the poetry of the Monterey Peninsula is to be found at Point Lobos State Reserve. The wind-twisted Monterey cypress, the soft sighs of pine, the azure water foaming milky white around dark rocks that host the miniature worlds of the tidepools—all say Monterey.

Farther south, travelers experience an exquisite fragility riding the thin ribbon of Highway 1 through Big Sur country, under the imposing brow of the Santa Lucia Mountains and along the precipitous cliffs overlooking the Pacific. Gradually, the landscape softens into something less wild, more idyllic. Just when you're thinking it's the perfect place for a fairy-tale castle— Shazam! There it is! San Simeon, William Randolph Hearst's fantasy made real. A concourse of gardens, classic pools, and mansions displaying a dazzling collection of art make San Simeon the wonder of the Central Coast. Nearby Cambria, a tiny coastal town in the pines, is a delightful country contrast.

Dune buggies wheel up and down the dramatic sand dunes of Pismo

Beach, where those little bubbles in the sand may mean you're onto something big. A Pismo clam can be the size of a fist. Take a Clam Taxi to the prime spots and go for your limit.

San Luis Obispo's history tour is a surprise, covering nearly every period and contributing culture of California history. Architecture ranges from adobe to Frank Lloyd Wright. To the east, rolling countryside provides pastoral scenes to inspire an old-fashioned Sunday drive, even on Mondays.

NOTICE TO CENTRAL COAST TRAVELERS:
Although Scenic Highway 1 between San Simeon and Big Sur is often closed due to slides, Hearst Castle and Cambria are always accessible via U.S. 101 and Highway 46. They are well worth the detour when necessary.

The Guest House   **(805) 481-9304**
120 Hart Lane, Arroyo Grande, CA 93420
(Off U.S. 101, seventeen miles south of San Luis Obispo)

Homesick New Englanders, look no further than The Guest House at Arroyo Grande. It was built in the 1850's by a sea captain from the east and bears an unmistakable resemblance to the homes he left behind. Present owners Mark Miller and James Cunningham have kept the flavor of old New England alive in the house. Stenciled wall designs, American primitives, Oriental rugs, and family heirlooms add to the mellow, inviting atmosphere. A crackling fire in the hearth and comfortable places to sit make the living room a haven for easy conversation. (The afternoon social hour often stretches on into evening!) Breakfast is appropriately hearty fare, served in the front parlor or out in the garden. For traditional Yankee hospitality at the sign of the pineapple, The Guest House is a classic.

Cat in residence; no pets, children, or RV parking; full breakfast; afternoon refreshments; city park in turn-of-the-century village of Arroyo Grande; airport pickup (San Luis Obispo). 10% midweek discount.

Room	Bed	Bath	Entrance	Floor	Daily Rates S - D	(EP)
A	1Q	Shd*	Main	2	$40-$50	($10)
B	1D	Shd*	Main	2	$40-$50	($10)
C	1D	Shd	Main	1	$40-$50	($10)

Duane & Miriam Benell   **(805) 927-3112**
340 Weymouth, Cambria, CA 93428
(Just east of Highway 1)

The Benells look forward to spending the summers in their lovely Cambria home, and it's no wonder. They are just seven miles south of Hearst Castle, two blocks from Moonstone Beach, and within walking distance of charming Cambria village. The guest room is on the ground level, and the living-dining area is on the upper level with a view of the ocean. Having greatly enjoyed B&Bs abroad, hosts are pleased to extend hospitality to foreign visitors traveling in California. The Benells are in residence June through Labor Day. B&B is available the rest of the year with *advance reservations* by calling (213) 695-5431 or writing 12002 Beverly Drive, Whittier, CA 90601.

No pets or smoking; one or two children under twelve OK; full breakfast; small RV parking; TV and fireplace upstairs. 10% discount for two or more nights; EP rate is $5 for younger children. Advance reservations *essential* year-round for Hearst Castle tours.

Room	Bed	Bath	Entrance	Floor	Daily Rates S - D	(EP)
A	2T or 1K	Pvt	Main	1G	$30-$40	($10)

Reginald & Doris Dickson **(805) 927-8193**
1954 Langton, Cambria, CA 93428
(Off Ardath Drive)

The Dicksons' contemporary home stands on a forested hill about a mile from the ocean. The front yard is a flower and rock garden reminiscent of those in the hosts' native England. B&B accommodations are on the lower level as you enter the house. In effect, guests have a separate apartment. There is a combination sleeping, living, and dining area with luxurious carpeting, a large brick fireplace, and a wet bar. A short hallway connects this area to the private bath. Part of the Dicksons' graciousness is in making guests feel comfortable enough to do as they please. People are welcome to visit with them upstairs or indulge the need for restful privacy. Things to do close by include exploring the English-styled village of Cambria, walking on the beach, winetasting in small family wineries, and touring Hearst Castle. For lodging of exceptional quality and value, the Dicksons' B&B is as fine as they come.

No pets, children under twelve, or RV parking; smoking on decks only; TV; fireplace; wet bar; large front deck on main floor, small one at back of guest quarters. $5 extra charge for one-night stays.

Room	Bed	Bath	Entrance	Floor	Daily Rates S - D	(EP)
A	2T or 1K	Pvt	Main	1	$45-$50	($10)

D'Urbano Bed & Breakfast　　　　　　　　　　　　**(805) 927-8145**
P.O. Box 1516, Cambria, CA 93428
(Off Ardath Drive)

　　　From this wooded coastal site, you can peek at the ocean through the pines. It's very quiet and uncrowded, a perfect setting for the dear little Cape Cod house and the D'Urbanos' warm B&B hospitality. Don and Desi's special touches give the interior a certain homey feeling. At the top of the stairs, cozy bedrooms with sloped ceilings await B&B guests. Gathering around the living room fireplace is popular on chilly evenings. Casual hosts welcome you to enjoy their home as your own. A *friendlier* stop along the coast you'll never find.

　　　No pets or smoking; children over ten by arrangement; good places to walk or jog close by; fifteen minutes to Hearst Castle.

Room	Bed	Bath	Entrance	Floor	Daily Rates S - D	(EP)
A	2T	Pvt	Main	2	$25-$40	($15)
B	1D	Pvt	Main	2	$25-$40	($15)

New Davenport Bed & Breakfast
Davenport, CA 95017
(Nine miles north of Santa Cruz)

(408) 425-1818
or 426-4122

The New Davenport Bed & Breakfast is located in one of Davenport's original old buildings, just across the Coast Highway from the ocean. Four bright, comfortable rooms, furnished with antique beds and oak dressers, are available to B&B travelers. Delicious breakfasts and lunches are served next door at the New Davenport Cash Store (pictured). This landmark also houses a pottery, gift, and craft gallery. Dinner is served on Friday, Saturday, and Sunday nights. Weekend festivities often include live music and a lively crowd. The New Davenport is an ideal getaway from the Bay Area. Though the trip is short, there's a wonderfully remote feeling about the place. And when you don't have to spend hours driving, there's much more time for fun.

No pets; no children under twelve; no smoking in rooms; bus service from Santa Cruz. Additional rooms are available on the second story of the main (Cash Store) building, most with ocean views. Rates range from $70-$85 for two. 15% discount Sunday-Thursday nights, November 1 to April 1.

Room	Bed	Bath	Entrance	Floor	Daily Rates S - D	(EP)
A	1D	Pvt	Main	1G	$50	
B	1D	Pvt	Main	1G	$50	
C	1Q	Pvt	Main	1G	$55	
D	1D	Pvt	Main	1G	$50	

Bayview House   **(805) 528-3098**
1070 Santa Lucia Avenue, Baywood Park, CA 93402
(On Morro Bay)

You'd have to search a long time to find a spot more peaceful than Bayview House, home of Jack and Frieda Murphy. The waxing tide brings the sound of lapping waves, and birds abound with their varied sounds (over two hundred species sited to date); other than that, it's profoundly quiet. A ground floor apartment offers absolute privacy. Unusually spacious and impeccably furnished, it consists of a living room, dining area, bedroom, bath, fully equipped kitchen, and a private deck that faces the bay. Deluxe breakfasts at Bayview House include such specialties as homemade sausages and bread; Frieda not only bakes the bread, but grinds the grain for it by hand. This is a place to savor some of life's simpler pleasures: gorgeous sunsets, miles of beaches and sand dunes, great birdwatching, hiking in state parks, and a quaint fishing village. It's the central coast at its most relaxing.

Dog in residence; no pets; full breakfast; TV; living room with sofa bed; kitchen; deck; some Dutch and Indonesian spoken; bus transportation; airport pickup (San Luis Obispo County).

Room	Bed	Bath	Entrance	Floor	Daily Rates S - D	(EP)
A	1D & 1Q	Pvt	Sep	1G	$45-$55	($10)

Darken Downs Equestre-Inn   **(805) 467-3589**
Star Route, Box 4562, San Miguel, CA 93451
(Nine miles northeast of Paso Robles)

After many years in the Oakland area, Kenneth and Darlene Ramey are making a dream come true by settling in the horse country near Paso Robles. Darlene's expertise with horses and Kenneth's love of writing are being realized here. They invite people to come with their horses to enjoy what this new compound has to offer. There's a "luxurious" barn, as well as paddocks, a training ring, and an arena (all fenced). Horse trailers can be easily unloaded, and horses will have outstanding accommodations. People, too (with or without horses), will be well taken care of in the Rameys' Spanish-style ranch home. Two bedrooms are available to guests, one with twin beds and the other with a double antique sleigh bed. For a taste of true western hospitality in the wide open countryside, visit Darken Downs Equestre-Inn.

Small poodle in residence; no pets; smoking outside only; facilities for guests' horses; wine-tasting and touring in surrounding Paso Robles wine country; airport pickup (Paso Robles). Evenings best to phone for reservations.

Room	Bed	Bath	Entrance	Floor	Daily Rates S - D	(EP)
A	2T	Shd*	Main	1G	$35-$40	
B	1D	Shd*	Main	1G	$35-$40	

Bob & Jane Rynders' Bed & Breakfast Cabin   **(415) 879-0319**
P.O. Box 478, Pesdadero, CA 94060
(Near Butano State Park)

Nestled in the ferns and redwoods alongside picturesque Butano Creek, this woodland hideaway is a unique blend of comfort and charm. Relax in a cozy sitting room (which can double as a second bedroom), warmed by the pot-bellied stove and soothing color scheme. From the bedroom, enjoy the embrace of a huge redwood tree just outside the patio door. Browse the book nook, which has books for every taste—from Lady Murasaki to Ian Fleming. Feel like a hike? Then you'll want to take the trail leading from the cabin to a waterfall that any outdoor lover should not miss. Amateur botanists will marvel at the profusion of flora, and field guides have been thoughtfully provided. The primitive gravel road that winds its way through the forest to this sequestered retreat (you will need directions) is an appropriate prelude for the rest and relaxation you can expect at the hospitable hands of the Rynders.

No pets or RV parking; full breakfast; TV; kitchenette with essentials for simple cooking; deck; barbecue; some knowledge of Japanese language and culture. Two-night minimum on holiday weekends.

Room	Bed	Bath	Entrance	Floor	Daily Rates S - D	(EP)
A	2Q	Pvt	Sep	1G	$50	($10)

Bruce & Susan Bangert (408) 476-1906
2501 Paul Minnie Avenue, Santa Cruz, CA 95062
(One quarter-mile from Highway 1, Soquel Avenue Exit)

The Bangerts' inviting old farmhouse seems to welcome you as you draw near, and once inside, the feeling is complete. Restored with loving care over the last few years, the house stands ready to delight any traveler lucky enough to discover it. The decor centers around the many works of art collected by the Bangerts. A dazzling array of ceramic pieces have been selected by Bruce, former head of the Ceramics Department at UC Santa Cruz. Two artists-in-residence work in the studio behind the house, where visitors can examine their wares. The Bangerts have a baby grand piano, a warm patio, and a relaxing deck that they enjoy sharing. Two gable-roofed bedrooms with an adjoining half-bath are available to B&B guests. The truly welcoming atmosphere, along with some nice surprises, have turned many guests into friends.

Dog in residence; TV; refrigerator and barbecue available; shared full bath on first floor; bus transportation.

Room	Bed	Bath	Entrance	Floor	Daily Rates S - D	(EP)
A	1D	Shd	Main	2	$35	
B	1D	Shd	Main	2	$35	

Heron House   **(408) 429-8963**
606 Graham Hill Road, Santa Cruz, CA 95060
(One mile from junction of Highways 1 and 17)

   Heron House was originally designed as an artist's studio and retains
many of the qualities that might nurture artistic expression. It is an exceptionally private, quiet 600-square-foot space that includes a living area, fully
equipped kitchen, bath, and a sleeping alcove with a beautiful brass bed. The
interior is kiln-dried redwood, with an open-beamed ceiling, hardwood floor,
Oriental rug, Franklin stove, and bay window seat. Hosts Anne and Dale
Easley make sure that a fire is laid prior to your arrival, and the hot tub is
ready for your exclusive use during your stay. The forested setting is often
sunny, providing a superb spot to relax on the deck overlooking a wooded
canyon where the great blue heron nests from late winter to late summer. They
are magnificent to hear and watch. Heron House is a cozy, romantic, soothing
place to steal away to for a few days. When you need to refresh your spirits, or
your relationship, give it a try.
   No smoking in sleeping area; supplies for breakfast and light cooking
provided (can be supplemented by guests for serious cooking); cable TV;
futon; deck with hot tub; Weber grill available; two miles from ocean; French
spoken. $15 extra charge for one-night stays on weekends (in season); $450
weekly rate. **KNIGHTTIME PUBLICATIONS SPECIAL RATE: 15% discount Sunday-Thursday nights September-April with this book (two-night
minimum).

Room	Bed	Bath	Entrance	Floor	Daily Rates S - D	(EP)
A	1D	Pvt	Sep	1	$75	

Dunmovin   **(408) 728-4154**
1006 Hecker Pass Road, Watsonville, CA 95076
(Between Watsonville and Gilroy)

     Located at the top of Hecker Pass, Ruth and Don Wakefield's rambling gray Tudor home is set on twenty-two acres with a giant redwood grove, Christmas trees, and free-roaming wildlife. The view from the many-windowed home is unsurpassed (a delight during breakfast in the family room). Dunmovin is situated partway between Santa Cruz and Monterey at such an elevation that you can see both towns plus the entire Monterey Bay. There is a separate wing for guests. Room A can be closed off and entered by its own door. Room B can be added to the accommodations and share the bath, ideal for couples traveling together. Room C is great for families; it's removed from the main part of the house and is entered separately. It has long, built-in twin beds and a queen-sized sofa bed. If you stay at Dunmovin, you can partake of the U-Pick fruits and vegetables of Watsonville; go wine-tasting at the small, family-run Hecker Pass wineries; and discover the many thrills of the Monterey Bay area.

     Dog, cat, and two peacocks on premises; no pets in house; full breakfast; TV; near Mount Madonna Park with restaurant and golf course; airport pickup (Watsonville). If bath is shared by Rooms A and B, rate is $45 per room.

Room	Bed	Bath	Entrance	Floor	Daily Rates S - D	(EP)
A	1Q	Pvt	Sep	1	$45-$55	
B	1D	Shd*		1	$45	
C	2T & 1Q	Pvt	Sep	1	$45	($10)

If you reject the food, ignore the customs, fear the religion, and avoid the people, you might better stay home. You are like a pebble thrown into water; you become wet on the surface, but you are never a part of the water.

—James A. Michener

Voyage, travel, and change of place impart vigour.

—Seneca

San Francisco
& the
Bay Area

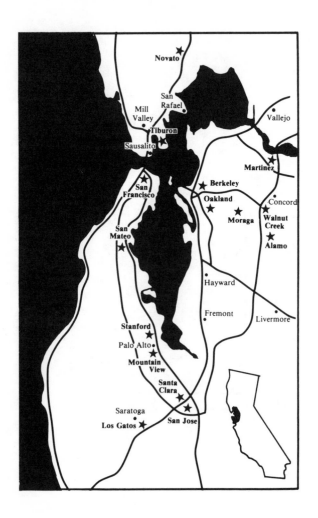

When you hear the clang of a cable car and the moan of a foghorn, you know where you are. San Francisco is like nowhere else, a city for all senses. Bounded on three sides by water, the feathery touch of sea mist is a pleasant certainty. Views from its famous hills—Telegraph, Russian, Nob, and Twin Peaks—are feasts for the eyes. Delicate, mysterious aromas arising from Chinatown contrast with the sharp sea smells of Fisherman's Wharf. Taste buds are tempted by over twenty-six hundred restaurants with an astounding choice of menus—Basque, Moroccan, Hungarian, Greek, Armenian, Swiss, Jewish, Indian, Chinese, Japanese, Filipino, Korean, Italian, Scandinavian, Mexican, Spanish. Truly, San Francisco is a city to savor.

The City is really several. One out of every seven San Franciscans is either foreign-born or a first-generation citizen. San Francisco streets belong to the neighborhoods, ethnic communities whose diverse customs and lifestyles make San Francisco more than the sum of its parts. Whether you are a resolute explorer or a dawdling gadabout, the streets of San Francisco are guaranteed to fascinate.

Crossing the Golden Gate Bridge, travelers are often surprised to find themselves in a spot of wilderness, the Marin headlands. Hiking the headlands is exhilarating. The intense blue of the bay, often dotted with sailboats, and hills that can be either spring green or summer gold have a lucid radiance.

Hiking the streets of Sausalito is equally heady, although in quite a different way. This Marin town is a favorite for window-shoppers and trend-spotters. Go with the flow, if only for an afternoon. Only slightly farther north, Mt. Tamalpais offers a more challenging hike as well as an unforgettable view. Muir Woods, at its foot, is a refuge of redwood and fern.

The Other Bridge (the Bay) takes you straight to Oakland, where the Oakland Museum answers more questions about California than you ever thought to ask. And Oakland must be one of the few cities in the country with a downtown saltwater lake, Lake Merritt.

Just south of the City is the Peninsula. The cities of Palo Alto and Menlo Park bustle at the base of oak-studded foothills. Many people have found their way to San Jose, one of the nation's fastest-growing cities. But not everyone has found the way to the hidden wine country surrounding it. More than fifty small to medium-sized wineries flourish in the Santa Clara Valley. Tours and tastings are unhurried and homey. The pastoral atmosphere may seem a world away from cosmopolitan San Francisco, but it's a mere fifty miles or so. In the Bay Area you can enjoy both.

Ruth Feldman
22 Gary Way, Alamo, CA 94507
(Two miles north of Danville, off I-680)

(415) 837-9038

Alamo sits almost at the foot of Mount Diablo, the highest peak and state park in the Bay Area. Nearby historic Danville is a remarkable restoration of a former stagecoach stop. It's a town for strolling around, shopping, and dining in the hotel known for fine cuisine and early California memorabilia. For a change of pace, Ruth's home and yard have an atmosphere of solitude and park-like serenity. There's a swimming pool, a garden, ponds with waterfalls, and an old-fashioned swing. Guest quarters are in a separate wing of the house, with a peaceful view, a brass bed, healthy plants, artwork, and a collection of exotic baskets. Blackberries from Oregon and strawberries from the back yard are made into preserves by Ruth and included in her breakfast specialties. People seeking respite here are likely to be pleased beyond their expectations.

Cat in residence; no dogs; no smoking preferred; TV; swimming pool; some German and Spanish spoken; good connections by BART to airports, San Francisco, Berkeley, and elsewhere. Host can recommend (and get advance tickets for) such local specialties as the Concord Pavilion, plays in San Francisco, and the elephant seals at Año Nuevo State Reserve.

Room	Bed	Bath	Entrance	Floor	Daily Rates S - D	(EP)
A	1D	Pvt	Main	1G	$30-$35	($5)

Ward Street House   **(415) 843-4188**
2201 Ward Street, Berkeley, CA 94705
(Above Shattuck Avenue, near Telegraph)

At a glance you can tell you'll be comfortable and secure in Sue Huestis's home on Ward Street. The large, brown-shingled house has a welcoming look. It's located on a quiet, tree-lined street in the South Campus area of Berkeley. Three pleasant upstairs guest rooms share a split bath. Breakfast is served in a charming, sun-filled dining area where international visitors enjoy sharing experiences over perfectly brewed "Berkeley-style" coffee and croissants. Fresh seasonal fruit completes the meal. Guests appreciate the relaxed atmosphere and the convenience of Ward Street House. Nearby are the UC campus, famous Telegraph Avenue, and excellent BART and bus service. Altogether, it's a combination that could suit your needs exactly.

No pets or children; TV; good airport connections. Rooms A and C have sinks; C has a sitting room with twin beds and a dressing room/closet. Brochure available.

Room	Bed	Bath	Entrance	Floor	Daily Rates S - D	(EP)
A	1D	Shd	Main	2	$30-$40	
B	1T & 1D	Shd	Main	2	$30-$40	($10)
C	2T & 1D	Shd	Main	2	$40-$50	($10)

Quinta Louisa   **(408) 354-6067**
18710 Bear Creek Road, Los Gatos, CA 95030
(Five minutes from downtown Los Gatos)

As you head for the Santa Cruz Mountains from Los Gatos, you soon
come to Bear Creek Road. It's a winding country road with scenery of woods
and vineyards. Quinta Louisa is half hidden, like a tree house. View a
fascinating collection of sculptures that line the inviting paths through the
grounds, which have been left in their natural state. Frank and Geri deMoss
offer guests the top floor of their home. There's a bedroom with queen sofa
bed, a bath, and a sitting area. Wood paneling, exposed beams, lots of windows, intriguing art objects gathered over years of travels, a wood-burning
stove, and a profound peacefulness—all convey a warm, country feeling. It's
hard to believe that bustling Los Gatos is only minutes away, with antique
shops, fine restaurants, an art movie house, and Old Town to tempt you out
of seclusion. At Quinta Louisa, the choices are all yours.

No pets; older children OK; smoking outside only; full or Continental
breakfast served on deck seasonally; kitchen privileges; swimming pool
(unheated); nearby golfing arranged by hosts; RV camping overnight (no
hookups) is $10. Sitting area with double sofa bed available at $25 with shared
bath. Alternate phone number: (408) 395-5050 (Frank). 10% discount to
AARP members.

Room	Bed	Bath	Entrance	Floor	Daily Rates S - D	(EP)
A	1Q	Pvt	Main	2	$35-$45	

Home Acre (415) 228-0227
2 Wanda Way, Martinez, CA 94553
(One and one-half miles south of Highway 4, Martinez Exit)

Jim and Meg Thomas's acre is part of the original ranch of John Muir, whose nearby home and grave are major attractions in the area. Sharing the acre with the hosts' comfortable, ranch-style home are fruit trees, flower and vegetable gardens, and a swimming pool. Their yard backs up to Alhambra Creek. The Redwood Regional Park system in the surrounding hills offers extensive hiking trails, many with exceptional views. Within half an hour are the Napa Valley, Mount Diablo, and San Francisco (by BART). History buffs will appreciate the stories Meg tells of the Bolbones Indians, John Muir, and other past inhabitants of this intriguing area. As a guest, you'll sample a taste of history when you're served a breakfast such as the Muir family might have enjoyed a hundred years ago.

Dog and cat in residence; smoking outside only; full breakfast; TV; kitchen privileges by arrangement; swimming pool; living room with fireplace for guests; extra bed; some Spanish spoken; airport pickup at extra charge (Buchanan, Oakland, San Francisco).

Room	Bed	Bath	Entrance	Floor	Daily Rates S - D	(EP)
A	1D	Shd*	Main	1G	$30-$40	($5)
B	1Q	Shd*	Main	1G	$30-$40	($5)

49

Frank & Virginia Hallman   **(415) 376-4318**
309 Constance Place, Moraga, CA 94556
(Five miles from Orinda BART station and Freeway 24)

At the Hallmans' Moraga home, you can have the best of both worlds while visiting the Bay Area. You can take off to "do" San Francisco in the ideal (car-less) fashion, then scoot back across the bay to the quiet luxury of this tastefully appointed home. The Hallmans will see that you have all the restorative comforts you need. There's a large pool and redwood hot tub in a private garden setting. Guest rooms are particularly pleasing. Moraga is usually sunny and is centrally located to many places of interest in the Bay Area. Hosts will help you find your way to the City, Berkeley, Napa Valley, Muir Woods, and elsewhere.

Two cats in residence; no pets, young children, or smoking; full breakfast optional; TV (B); swimming pool; hot tub; living room with fireplace for guests; five miles to JFK University, ten to UC Berkeley, twelve to Mills College; network of hiking trails through Moraga and Lafayette, as well as other East Bay regional parks, nearby; bus and BART service; airport connections from San Francisco and Oakland. Ask about weekly and family rates.

Room	Bed	Bath	Entrance	Floor	Daily Rates S - D	(EP)
A	1Q	Shd*	Main	1G	$35-$40	($10)
B	1Q	Shd*	Main	1G	$35-$40	($10)

The Alvin House   **(415) 964-3690**
2481 Alvin Street, Mountain View, CA 94043   **or 321-5195**
(Off U.S. 101, near Middlefield and San Antonio Roads)

It took great imagination and flair to convert this small Eichler home in suburban Mountain View to its present state. The exterior reveals nothing of the totally pleasing environment inside. A feeling of light and openness is derived from skylights and windows, open-beamed ceilings, delicate colors, and greenery in the house and landscaped yard. You walk on plush carpeting, sit on comfortable sofas, and snuggle under down comforters at The Alvin House. Play the antique baby grand Steinway if you like, or maybe throw a barbecue. Feel like a good soak in the Jacuzzi? Sliding glass doors from each bedroom lead to the yard and spa. You're most welcome to enjoy all that this elegant home has to offer—which is considerable. Some people stop over-night, while others take the whole house for a few days or several weeks. Host Scott Young likes for guests to consider The Alvin House a home away from home in every sense.

No pets or children; no smoking in bedrooms; full breakfast; com-plimentary wine; fully equipped kitchen; barbecue entertainment area; cable TV in two rooms. An extra room with twin bed can share bath with Room B at $35. **KNIGHTTIME PUBLICATIONS SPECIAL RATE: 10% discount with this book.

Room	Bed	Bath	Entrance	Floor	Daily Rates S - D	(EP)
A	2T or 1K	Pvt	Main	1G	$55	
B	1Q	Pvt	Main	1G	$55	

Faye & Robert Abbey   **(415) 892-5478**
55 Grande Vista, Novato, CA 94947
(Twenty-eight miles north of Golden Gate Bridge)

Novato is the northernmost city in Marin County and best known to some as the site of the annual Renaissance Pleasure Faire. Its location in the "Valley of Gentle Seasons" gives it a mild, healthful climate. Faye and Robert Abbey live in an older, well-groomed neighborhood. Their huge back yard is a beautiful landscape of flowers, ferns, and trees, with sitting areas for enjoying the park-like environment. Three bedrooms on the main floor and a suite on the upper floor comprise the B&B accommodations. A front room (A) is cheerfully decorated in red and white; the one across the hall (B) is done in peach with ivory lace and ruffles; an orchid bedroom (C) is furnished with "Granny's" antiques. The large master suite (D) offers complete privacy and a balcony with a view of the back yard. The Abbeys' home is an appealing place to stay, and its location poises the traveler for a foray into the Sonoma Wine Country, San Francisco, or Marin County's unique towns, parks, and coastline.

Bicycles available for nearby trails; TV (in suite and family room); hot tub; living room with fireplace available to guests; fully equipped (second) kitchen adjoining Room B can be used by guests at an extra charge.

Room	Bed	Bath	Entrance	Floor	Daily Rates S - D	(EP)
A	2T	Shd*	Main	1	$30-$40	
B	1Q	Pvt	Sep	1	$30-$40	
C	1T	Shd*	Main	1	$30	
D	1K	Pvt	Main	2	$50	

Rockridge Bed & Breakfast   **(415) 655-1223**
5428 Thomas Avenue, Oakland, CA 94618
(Near College and Broadway)

Rockridge B&B is a 1915 two-story stucco home in a pleasant north Oakland neighborhood. Hosts Bob and Jean Huston have restored the downstairs woodwork to the original gumwood finish, and its natural warmth imbues the interior. Two large upstairs bedrooms accommodate B&B guests. The back room (A) overlooks the garden, and the other room has a bed with a canopy. Your kindly hosts can direct you to nearby shopping streets, public transportation, or anywhere you need to go. A good choice for its convenience and comfort, Rockridge B&B feels, well, just like home.

No pets or smoking; BART and buses nearby; occasional airport pickup and good airport connections (Oakland, San Francisco). Brochure available.

Room	Bed	Bath	Entrance	Floor	Daily Rates S - D	(EP)
A	1T & 1D	Shd	Main	2	$25-$35	($5)
B	1T & 1D	Shd	Main	2	$25-$35	($5)

Jessie & Pete Taylor   **(415) 531-2345**
59 Chelton Lane, Oakland, CA 94611
(Oakland Hills)

The Taylors love sharing their home, which is set on a quiet lane in the hills above Oakland and the San Francisco Bay. Here you'll be assured of a gracious welcome and a good night's rest—but that's only the beginning. For these generous-spirited hosts, taking special care of guests is a top priority. Two lovely guest rooms and a bath on the lower level of the house can be closed off for an extra measure of privacy. You may have breakfast on the front deck enclosed by a soothing Japanese garden, or on the rear deck facing the bay. View jewel-like San Francisco by night from your bedroom, the living room, or the deck. Three islands (Yerba Buena, Alcatraz, and Angel) and two bridges (Bay and Golden Gate) are visible by day. Need I say more?

No RV parking; full breakfast; TV; decks. Two parties traveling together may share the bath or use an additional bath at the top of the stairs.

Room	Bed	Bath	Entrance	Floor	Daily Rates S - D	(EP)
A	2T	Pvt	Main	LL	$25-$35	($10)
B	1D	Pvt	Main	LL	$25-$35	($10)

Aurora Manor   **(415) 564-2480**
1328 Sixteenth Avenue, San Francisco, CA 94122
(Just south of Golden Gate Park and UC Medical Center)

Travelers seeking informal lodgings with an international flavor find it easy to make themselves at home in Aurora Manor, owned and operated by Saskia Grabowski. Her Dutch background and European contacts draw many visitors from abroad who appreciate the inviting atmosphere and Saskia's expertise in helping them get acquainted with "everyone's favorite city." There are three bedrooms for guests on the main floor and two on the lower, plus three shared baths, kitchen and laundry access, and a living room with a fireplace. Coffee and tea are always available, and afternoon hors d'oeuvres and sherry are offered. In moments of leisure, guests may enjoy reading or conversation in the comfortable living room. A friendly, generous spirit marks the hospitality awaiting you at Aurora Manor.

No pets; full breakfast; TV in each room; kitchen and laundry privileges; refreshments available; Dutch, German, French, and some Norwegian spoken; good public transportation and airport connections. Master Card and Visa accepted; Telex 5522372 1P HOWD.

Room	Bed	Bath	Entrance	Floor	Daily Rates S - D	(EP)
A	1T & 1D	Shd*	Main	2	$32-$38	
B	2T	Shd*	Main	2	$32-$38	
C	1D	Shd*	Main	2	$32-$38	
D	1D	Shd*	Main	1	$32-$38	
E	1D	Shd*	Main	1	$32-$38	

Bed & Breakfast Near the Park   **(415) 753-3574**
1387 Sixth Avenue, San Francisco, CA 94122
(Two blocks from Golden Gate Park and UC Medical Center)

John and Alice Micklewright are the second owners of this 1910 Edwardian-style home. It is quite handsome in appearance, from the unusual sloped roof to the extensive interior woodwork, which is all original. The house feels rich, solid, and handcrafted. The upper floor is exclusively for guests. It has been painted, carpeted, and furnished with obvious care. Room A is light and airy, with an adjoining kitchen and a small deck. Room B is painted a regal-looking blue, and has a cheery, flower-filled window box. The front bedroom (C) is the most spacious; it's done in dusty rose and has a large bay window. Guests share a split bath with a clawfoot tub and skylights. Accommodations are tailor-made for a group of up to seven people, but unrelated parties also find the arrangement convenient. Well-traveled hosts welcome the opportunity of getting to know new people in their own home.

Dog in residence; no pets or smoking; kitchen (A); extra bed; good public transportation and airport connections; French spoken. Weekly and monthly rates off season (November-April).

Room	Bed	Bath	Entrance	Floor	Daily Rates S - D	(EP)
A	1D	Shd*	Main	2	$35-$45	
B	1D	Shd*	Main	2	$35-$45	
C	2T or 1K	Shd*	Main	2	$35-$45	($10)

Carl Street Unicorn House   **(415) 753-5194**
156 Carl Street, San Francisco, CA 94117
(Upper Haight district, near Cole)

Nowhere is the City's vibrancy felt more keenly than in the Haight. Here the unexpected and offbeat find expression in a melange of quirky shops, small cafes, and people of all descriptions. Golden Gate Park, with its museums, aquarium, biking and walking paths, is within walking distance. Carl Street Unicorn House is set amidst this festive neighborhood. Miriam Weber, a resident since 1956, fits right in. Her small Victorian home is a tribute to her interest in music, the arts, and, of course, unicorns. (Ask to see the "Unicorner.") She occupies the top floor, and guests reside in a pleasant room on the main floor where a marvelous San Francisco quilt is on display. All in all, it's a setting guaranteed to warm the body and the soul.

Cat in residence; no pets, children, smoking, or RV parking; good public transportation. $3 extra charge for one-night stays; 10% discount for a week.

Room	Bed	Bath	Entrance	Floor	Daily Rates S - D	(EP)
A	1D	Shd	Main	1	$30-$40	

Casa Arguello (415) 752-9482
225 Arguello Boulevard, San Francisco, CA 94118
(Presidio Heights, between California and Lake)

Mrs. Emma Baires makes her B&B guests feel right at home in Casa Arguello, a large, two-floor flat with spacious, immaculate rooms. The view from each room is a constant reminder that you couldn't be anywhere *but* San Francisco. Presidio Heights is a safe residential area within easy walking distance of shops on Sacramento Street, Laurel Village, and Clement Street. Excellent restaurants and public transportation are also close by. It isn't surprising that Mrs. Baires has a lot of return visitors. The cheerfulness of Casa Arguello lingers long after you have left.

No pets; TV (D); large living room with TV for guests; Spanish spoken; good airport connections. Two-night minimum preferred; $5 extra charge for one-night stays. A two-room master suite is also available at $75.

Room	Bed	Bath	Entrance	Floor	Daily Rates S - D	(EP)
A	1D	Shd*	Main	3	$38	
B	1D	Shd*	Main	3	$38	
C	2T	Shd*	Main	3	$38	
D	1K	Pvt	Main	3	$45	

A Country Cottage   **(415) 931-3083**
P.O. Box 349, San Francisco, CA 94101
(#5 Dolores Terrace)

   Discovering A Country Cottage is like finding a surprise tucked away in a pocket you didn't know you had. Dolores Terrace is a hidden little pocket just off Dolores Street and very close to downtown. Susan and Richard Kreibich have restored this small, brown-shingled house to top condition. The exterior has modern lines; the interior is crisp, clean, and loaded with country comfort. The house is larger than it appears. The Kreibichs live on the main floor and serve breakfast in their sunny kitchen. B&B guests are accommodated downstairs, where there are three bedrooms, a bath, a pretty patio with trees and birds, and a separate entrance. The carpeted rooms have beautiful brass or oak beds and country antiques. Hosts also operate "American Family Inn," a reservation service with private homes all over the City. If you're making late reservations or looking for a particular kind of lodging, chances are they can help. For a taste of quiet country living in the midst of San Francisco, their cottage is a winner.

   No children; full breakfast; complimentary wine; patio; travel information provided; wholesale shopping tours arranged; German spoken; no RV parking and limited car parking; good public transportation and airport connections.

Room	Bed	Bath	Entrance	Floor	Daily Rates S - D	(EP)
A	1Q	Shd*	Sep	LL	$45-$55	
B	1Q	Shd*	Sep	LL	$45-$55	
C	1D	Shd*	Sep	LL	$45-$55	

Dorothy Franzblau   **(415) 564-7686**
2331 Ninth Avenue, San Francisco, CA 94116
(Just south of Golden Gate Park and UC Medical Center)

Dorothy Franzblau's home is on an upper street of Forest Hill, one of San Francisco's many interesting neighborhoods. Some of its assets include exhilarating views, good places for walking and running, and proximity to the lively shops and restaurants near Ninth and Irving. Guests in Dorothy's home are treated with care. Breakfast is a potpourri of her special creations, and a snack awaits you in your private sitting room each night. The guest suite is a calm haven to return to after a busy day.

No pets; limited smoking; full breakfast; TV; extra bed; good public transportation; limited German, Hungarian, and French spoken. Call for reservations before 9:00 a.m. or after 3:30 p.m.

Room	Bed	Bath	Entrance	Floor	Daily Rates S - D	(EP)
A	2T	Pvt	Main	2	$35-$45	($15)

Jackie's Bed & Breakfast   **(415) 474-1076**
3 McCormick Street, San Francisco, CA 94109
(Off Pacific between Larkin and Hyde)

This deluxe garden apartment is hidden away on a quiet cul-de-sac near Nob Hill. It's a tranquil oasis for the busy traveler to return to after sampling the best of San Francisco. From Jackie's, all the choice spots are easy to reach by cable car, bus, or on foot. It's amazing how many excellent restaurants and specialty shops are within walking distance. Accommodations include a bedroom, dressing room, bath, kitchen, and living-dining area. Sliding glass doors open to a private garden where you'll find relaxing places to sit. Your thoughtful host provides all the amenities you could want—and many you haven't thought of—to make your stay in San Francisco truly exceptional.

No pets; children over five welcome; smoking in garden area only; full breakfast; completely stocked kitchen; living room sofa converts to extra double bed; good airport connections; French spoken. Small car parking at $3 per day; $10 extra charge for one-night stays; 10% discount for a week.

Room	Bed	Bath	Entrance	Floor	Daily Rates S - D	(EP)
A	1D	Pvt	Sep	LL	$60-$65	($15)

Lyon Street Bed & Breakfast (415) 552-4773
120 Lyon Street, San Francisco, CA 94117
(Near Panhandle of Golden Gate Park, at Oak)

Ruth and Eric Johnson live on the first two floors of their lovely Queen Anne Victorian home. The third floor apartment has been converted to a most inviting B&B accommodation. Several books on San Francisco Victorians have documented the house's interesting architectural history. The Johnsons have worked for years to renovate the structure to its original concept, and they've done a marvelous job. The guest floor has a bedroom, two sitting rooms, a kitchen, and a bath; it could easily accommodate up to four people. The location of Lyon Street B&B is both pleasant and convenient, allowing guests to reach many interesting places by bus, trolley, or on foot. Give Ruth a little advance notice and she'll serve you one of her large, farmhouse breakfasts. A warm and hospitable climate is yours when you visit the Johnsons on Lyon Street.

Two cats in residence; no pets; children welcome; no smoking preferred; extra charge for farmhouse breakfast; TV; kitchen; good airport connections.

Room	Bed	Bath	Entrance	Floor	Daily Rates S - D	(EP)
A	2Q	Pvt	Main	3	$60-$65	($10)

The Masonic Manor   **(415) 621-3365**
1468 Masonic, San Francisco, CA 94117
(Buena Vista Heights, near Frederick)

This magnificent English Tudor home was built in 1904 by a lumber baron, and the abundant use of redwood throughout the interior shows the fine craftsmanship of the period. A formal dining room is paneled with rare tigereye redwood, and an elaborate fireplace with carved figureheads graces the living room. On the second floor, two exquisite guest accommodations have the same designer showcase look as the rest of the house. The spacious Iris Suite is done in subtle shades of blue and lavender. You can peer at the ocean from behind large iris-appliqued curtains created by a local artist. Smaller but equally enchanting is the Orchid Room. It has a lace-canopied bed, orchid-appliqued curtains, a marble vanity sink, and a stairway leading to the Manor's garden spa. The Martins—Dianne, John, and Tyler—provide a warm welcome and all the comforts of home in the casual elegance of The Masonic Manor.

Smoking in common areas only; TV with movie channel (in family room), fireplace with logs, and garden spa for guests' use; full breakfast in formal dining room at 9 a.m. Excellent for honeymoons and special occasions. **KNIGHTTIME PUBLICATIONS SPECIAL RATE: 15% discount with this book.

Room	Bed	Bath	Entrance	Floor	Daily Rates S - D	(EP)
A	1K	Shd*	Main	2	$70	($10)
B	1Q	Shd*	Main	2	$60	($10)

Nancy's Bed & Breakfast   **(415) 431-5332**
125 Lyon Street, San Francisco, CA 94117
(Near Panhandle of Golden Gate Park, at Oak)

Nancy Derthick's attractive Victorian home is near Golden Gate Park and the revitalized Haight-Ashbury district. The private studio apartment with a complete kitchen and a view of the garden makes a good choice for travelers who are planning longer stays and would like the option of eating in occasionally. Plants and neutral colors mark the decor, and the quiet, off-street location adds to the relaxing atmosphere. Nancy can suggest some interesting neighborhood spots that you can walk to or tell you how to get most anywhere by public transportation. She particularly likes the Steinhart Aquarium and DeYoung Museum, both in the Park. Her B&B accommodation is convenient, private, and quiet—a winning combination in San Francisco.

No pets; smoking in garden only; complimentary sherry; full kitchen; good airport connections. Lower rates for extended stays.

Room	Bed	Bath	Entrance	Floor	Daily Rates S - D	(EP)
A	1Q	Pvt	Sep	1	$50	($10)

Riley's Bed & Breakfast   **(415) 731-0788**
1322-24 Sixth Avenue, San Francisco, CA 94122
(Between Irving & Judah, near Golden Gate Park and UC Med Center)

Riley's captures the spirit of a real home away from home in a 1908 antique-furnished Victorian. While neither grand nor luxurious, the refurbished guest rooms have strong appeal for their neat and tasteful simplicity. Host Bob Brown's easygoing manner and concern for his guests add to the homey, comfortable feeling that is sometimes hard to find in an unfamiliar city. He can point out interesting neighborhood spots, or tell you about some wonderful walks in the vicinity. One of his favorites is the five blocks to Golden Gate Park where you can visit the Steinhart Aquarium, de Young Museum, Strybing Arboretum, and more. Riley's is an agreeable place in every aspect, and I consider it quite a "find."

No pets or smoking; families welcome; kitchen privileges; split bathroom; good public transportation and airport connections. A and B are connecting rooms. Weekly accommodations available on a separate floor. Brochure available. 10% discount to AARP members.

Room	Bed	Bath	Entrance	Floor	Daily Rates S - D	(EP)
A	2T	Shd	Main	2	$30-$35	
B	1Q	Shd	Main	2	$40-$45	
C	1Q	Shd	Main	2	$40-$45	

Elizabeth Shore-Wilson   **(415) 346-8468**
2212 Divisadero, San Francisco, CA 94115
(Pacific Heights)

For a slice of the elegant life of old San Francisco, this Pacific Heights Victorian would be hard to top. Just walking around in this neighborhood you can catch some heady views of the City, note the distinctive architecture, and dawdle in a plethora of boutiques, cafes, and restaurants. Elizabeth, a native of New Zealand, is a concert singer. She is glad to share her grand piano with guests who are musically inclined. A large, high-ceilinged guest room is quiet and private; a modernized private bathroom is just across the hall. The entire house is kept in first-rate condition and offers the traveler an atmosphere of refined comfort.

No pets or children; full breakfast; TV; kitchen and laundry privileges by arrangement; good bus, taxi, and limousine service; German and French spoken.

Room	Bed	Bath	Entrance	Floor	Daily Rates S - D (EP)	
A	1Q	Pvt	Main	1	$65	

Ed & Monica Widburg (415) 564-1751
2007 Fifteenth Avenue, San Francisco, CA 94116
(South of Golden Gate Park and UC Medical Center)

The Widburgs' home has an individual charm of its own, both inside and out. Their wide, quiet street is elevated to allow striking views of the ocean and the Golden Gate. The rose-beige stucco home and landscaped yard have a look of understated elegance. European and Indonesian art objects, antiques, maps, and family heirlooms fit well into an interior graced with exquisite finishing details. At the front of the main floor, a bed/sitting room (A) and adjacent bath are available to guests. A room for a single traveler (B) is just off the hallway and, when occupied, shares the bath. Hosts sleep downstairs, so there's an extra degree of privacy. Large view windows across the back of the house make the dining and living rooms unusually pleasant. The Widburgs' European background contributes to their unfailing graciousness: they are not only well traveled but accustomed to hosting visitors from other countries. Bed and breakfast is a way of life to them, and sharing their special city by the sea is second nature.

Dog in residence; no pets, children, or smoking; TV (A); European languages spoken; good public transportation and airport connections.

Room	Bed	Bath	Entrance	Floor	Daily Rates S - D	(EP)
A	1Q	Shd*	Main	2	$40-$45	
B	1T	Shd*	Main	2	$35	

The Glen Eyrie **(408) 293-6247**
1275 Glen Eyrie Avenue, San Jose, CA 95125
(Willow Glen area, off I-280 and Meridian Avenue)

The Glen Eyrie, home of Betty and "Waddy" White, typifies the quiet graciousness of the tree-studded Willow Glen area. It is beautifully kept, and the decor throughout is fresh, colorful, and soothing to the senses. On one side of the house there are two bedrooms (A and B) with a connecting hallway and a private bath. (B is used only if a party needs both rooms.) Rich carpeting, delicate colors, and graceful furnishings make the rooms particularly appealing. An adjacent garden room, and indeed most of the house, is available for your relaxation. A separate lanai cottage behind the house (C) is a glorious retreat—truly a gem. It has a sitting/sleeping room with a fireplace, a private bath, and a patio/garden overlooking a picturesque creek. The Whites tailor their hospitality to the needs and schedule of each guest. In every respect, The Glen Eyrie is an outstanding spot.

Dog and three cats in residence; no pets; no smoking preferred; full breakfast; afternoon refreshments; TV; AC; airport pickup (San Jose). Inquire about family and weekly rates. **KNIGHTTIME PUBLICATIONS SPECIAL RATE: 10% discount with this book.

Room	Bed	Bath	Entrance	Floor	Daily Rates S - D	(EP)
A	1Q	Pvt	Main	1G	$50	
B	1D				$40	
C	1Q	Pvt	Sep	1G	$75	

Barbara & George Kievlan   **(408) 559-3828**
14497 New Jersey Avenue, San Jose, CA 95124
(Near Campbell, Los Gatos, and Highway 17)

Although you'd never guess it, this sprawling suburban home occupies part of the old Blossom Valley Ranch, and the historic ranch house still stands in the vicinity. The first thing you notice upon entering the spacious living room is an oversized fireplace that dominates the room, offering its warm glow when the weather's chilly. In warmer weather, the large family room and adjacent patio with pool are the usual gathering places. The Kievlans are very accommodating people. Their home conveys the feeling that you can truly do as you please, whether your urge is to socialize, do some light cooking, or spend some time alone. As a guest here, you'll soon feel like just blending into this comfortable household.

Dog in residence; no pets; smoking outside only; TV; AC; kitchen and laundry privileges; extra bed in room, $10; swimming pool; pool table; wheelchair access; airport pickup at extra charge (San Jose). Credit cards accepted; 2% discount for cash or travelers checks; weekly and seasonal rates.

Room	Bed	Bath	Entrance	Floor	Daily Rates S - D	(EP)
A	1K	Pvt	Sep	1G	$40-$50	
B	2T or 1K	Pvt	Sep	1G	$35-$40	
C	2T	Pvt	Sep	1G	$30-$35	

O'Neill's Private Accommodations   **(408) 996-1231**
11801 Sharon Drive, San Jose, CA 95129
(West San Jose, bordering Saratoga and Cupertino)

     The O'Neills offer something that is hard to find in the fast-paced Santa Clara Valley: exceptionally private, quiet, home-like accommodations for visitors. People they have hosted include business travelers who like privacy but are tired of hotels, relatives of families in the area, newlyweds who have held receptions in the huge back yard entertainment area, and newcomers who are looking for permanent housing. Choose between a large suite (bedroom, bath, living room) and a studio (bed/living room and bath). Each is delightfully furnished, carpeted, wallpapered, and equipped with refrigerator, coffee maker, telephone, cable TV, and other conveniences. Provisions for a Continental breakfast are supplied in each unit, so your schedule can be easily accommodated. People who have found their way to O'Neill's consider it a wonderful discovery.

     Full complement of amenities plus a double sofa bed ($5 extra to use) in each unit; AC in studio; large pool/patio area with cabana and barbecue facilities (private parties by arrangement). Brochure available. Credit cards accepted.

Room	Bed	Bath	Entrance	Floor	Daily Rates S - D	(EP)
A	1Q	Pvt	Sep	1G	$60	
B	1Q	Pvt	Sep	1G	$50	

SAN MATEO

The Palm House (415) 573-7256
1216 Palm Avenue, San Mateo, CA 94402
(A block east of El Camino Real, between 12th and 13th Avenues)

Alan and Marian Brooks have enjoyed creating The Palm House, and they're justifiably proud of it. Built in 1907, it's a picture-book home in a quiet residential area of San Mateo. The interior has a warm, European ambiance created by multi-paned windows and dark wooden panels and beams. Some of the stunning works of art on the walls were done by Alan, an accomplished and successful painter. B&B guests are treated to gracious breakfast service and sun-dried, 100% cotton sheets and towels. The Palm House is located within walking distance of shops and restaurants; San Francisco International Airport is a short ride away by bus or taxi. You can get to San Francisco, Stanford University, or the Pacific Ocean in less than thirty minutes, and all can be reached by public transportation. Alan and Marian wish to convey the spirit of English bed and breakfast to their guests—and you'll see a surprising bit of evidence to prove it.

Children welcome.

Room	Bed	Bath	Entrance	Floor	Daily Rates S - D	(EP)
A	1T & 1Q	Pvt	Main	2	$45-$50	($10)
B	1D	Pvt	Main	2	$40	

Madison Street Bed & Breakfast   **(408) 249-5541**
1390 Madison Street, Santa Clara, CA 95050
(Near Santa Clara University and San Jose Municipal Airport)

One doesn't necessarily associate the Santa Clara Valley with historic homes and genteel living, but that is exactly what you'll find at Theresa and Ralph Wigginton's completely restored Victorian on Madison Street. The result of their painstaking work is a unique lodging establishment with turn-of-the-century style and personal service. The high-ceilinged rooms are appointed with wallcoverings of authentic Victorian design, Oriental rugs, antique furnishings, brass beds, and one romantic four-poster. Deluxe breakfasts are served in a dining room that overlooks landscaped grounds with a pool, spa, and barbecue area. Hosts will try to accommodate your business or personal needs; they can arrange for such things as private meetings and intimate, home-cooked dinners. A most pleasant atmosphere for work or relaxation is yours at Madison Street Bed & Breakfast.

Smoking in common areas only; full breakfast; TV and VCR available; sink in C and D; robes provided; work desk with telephone; dry cleaning services; pool and spa; dinners (from a tantalizing menu!) for four to sixteen guests by arrangement; private meetings. Brochure available. Ask about weekly rates. **KNIGHTTIME PUBLICATIONS SPECIAL RATE: 10% discount with this book.

Room	Bed	Bath	Entrance	Floor	Daily Rates S - D	(EP)
A	1Q	Pvt	Main	1	$75	
B	1D	Pvt	Main	1	$65	
C	1D	Shd*	Main	1	$55	
D	1D	Shd*	Main	1	$55	
E	1D	Pvt	Sep	LL	$65	

The Oasting House (415) 321-5195
P.O. Box 4528, Stanford, CA 94305
(Between El Camino Real and I-280)

Staying at The Oasting House is my idea of Going First Class. Picture a country estate with private, automatic gates in a park-like setting. It is peaceful and tree-studded, with resident owls, quail, and mockingbirds. All this within reach of major freeways, peninsula attractions, and San Francisco? Hard to believe, but true. Wilheim Oasting, a German potato chip baron, built the Tyrolean house in the 1920's as a summer residence to which he would bring his entire family and staff of servants from San Francisco to escape the summer fog. Tricia, your host, has succeeded in making her home tasteful, luxurious, and extremely livable. The amenities provided for guests are too numerous to mention. Let me put it this way: If you have a hard time giving way to indulgence, you'd better go someplace else.

Dog and pet fowl outside; no pets or children; no smoking preferred; ranch-style breakfast with daily fresh eggs; TV in each room; laundry privileges; solar-heated swimming pool; patio and barbecue; sunken tub with Jacuzzi (B and C); refrigerator and dining area (A,D,F); bicycles available for nearby trails; German spoken; courtesy airport pickup (Palo Alto, San Francisco, San Jose). Two-night minimum. Unit E has a fully equipped kitchen and a separate entrance through French doors from patio/pool area.

Room	Bed	Bath	Entrance	Floor	Daily Rates S - D	(EP)
A	1Q	Pvt	Sep	1G	$65	
B	2T	Pvt	Main	2	$65	
C	1Q	Pvt	Main	2	$65	
D	2T or 1K	Pvt	Sep	1G	$65	
E	1Q	Pvt	Sep	1G	$75	

Bed & Breakfast in Tiburon (415) 435-0605
27 Old Landing Road, Tiburon, CA 94920
(Marin County, on San Francisco Bay)

Sandy Paul's ranch-style adobe home is set among trees and faces the bay. Deer roam freely through the yard. The home's interior is the essence of coziness and country charm. There's a small, private beachfront across the street where some guests favor sipping their morning coffee while contemplating the day ahead. A "must" for many visitors is the ferry trip from Tiburon to Angel Island (dock ten minutes away), a good place for hiking, picnicking, and riding bicycles. With the variety of unique shops and restaurants in Tiburon and nearby Sausalito—not to mention the stunning views of San Francisco from both spots—you don't really *need* to venture further to have a perfect holiday.

Cat in residence; no pets; good airport connections from San Francisco International by Marin Airporter.

Room	Bed	Bath	Entrance	Floor	Daily Rates S - D	(EP)
A	1D	Pvt	Main	1G	$35-$40	

Lois Martin   **(415) 934-8119**
2113 Blackstone Drive, Walnut Creek, CA 94598
(Near north entrance to Mount Diablo State Park)

Mount Diablo looms in the background of Lois Martin's rambling California ranch home. She calls it *"Gasthaus zum Bären,"* which translates to "Guest House at the Sign of the Bear." The California bear was first drawn by German explorer-artist Ludwig Choris; hence the California-German theme, which is carried out in the decor and the breakfast specialties. The Martins have made their home in various parts of the world. Art, artifacts, and furniture collected along the way add color and texture to the rooms. The atmosphere at the *Gasthaus* is friendly and easygoing. A shaded patio, a swimming pool, and a Jacuzzi are most inviting. In winter, a two-sided fireplace provides warmth to much of the living area. Let Lois know if you're attending an event at the Concord Pavilion (six miles away), and she can provide a special Pavilion Picnic—complete with silver goblets. Her hospitality shows imagination and care; you'll count yourself fortunate to be touched by it.

Dog and two cats in residence; no pets; families welcome; smoking outside only; full breakfast; TV available; kitchen privileges; extra beds; patio; barbecue; swimming pool; Jacuzzi; tennis rackets; bicycles; extra meals optional; Pavilion (or tailgate) picnics at extra charge; Heather Farms recreation area, hiking and biking trails, and an excellent golf course nearby; Spanish, German, and Italian spoken; good public transportation; airport pickup (Buchanan, Oakland, San Francisco). Room B is a choice between two rooms with different beds. 10% discount to seniors and families with children.

Room	Bed	Bath	Entrance	Floor	Daily Rates S - D	(EP)
A	2T or 1K	Pvt	Main	1G	$40-$45	($10)
B	2T or 1Q	Shd	Main	1G	$30-$35	($10)

How each friend represents a world in us, a world possibly not born until they arrive, and it is only by this meeting that a new world is born.

—Anaïs Nin

Do you know that conversation is one of the greatest pleasures in life? But it wants leisure.

—W. Somerset Maugham

Wine
Country

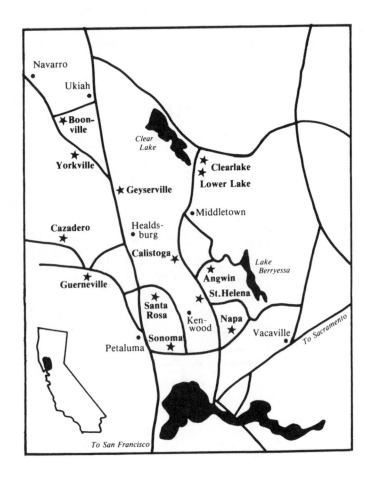

"How simple and frugal a thing is happiness: a glass of wine, a roast chestnut, a little brazier...." Everyone probably has a taste of simple happiness they would add to Nikos Kazantzakis's list, but most of us would keep a glass of wine at the top. The varied character of wine, its surprises and revelations, transform a day in the country into a celebration.

The Wine Country is not a homogeneous plain of back-to-back vineyards, but rather several unique valleys separated by peaks and foothills. Napa and Sonoma are the best known valleys, but wine connoisseurs are eagerly following up new leads in the Anderson, Russian River, and Ukiah Valleys as well. Each valley has its own community of wineries, often clustered like grapes on a vine, making traveling from one to another convenient.

A picnic is *de rigeur*. A loaf of bread, a chunk of cheese, deli delights, and the season's fruit provide the makings of a main event. A good place to stock up is the Rouge et Noir Cheese Shop in Petaluma, where they have been making Camembert, Brie, Schloss, and their special breakfast cheese for over a century. Petaluma's Victorians and "Iron Front" buildings, with their factory-made fronts of cast or sheet iron, are well worth a walking tour.

Sonoma Valley has many excellent wineries and some equally excellent sun-dappled settings for picnics. These vary from open valley vistas to shaded crannies near elusive streams. The back roads are also famous for pick-your-own fruits and vegetables.

Sonoma itself is a reflection of the past. Somehow the early California ranchos are real again, the Bear Flag Rebellion might erupt at any moment, and wasn't it just yesterday that Kit Carson dropped by the Blue Wing Inn? Jack London's ranch near Glen Ellen looks down on his beloved Valley of the Moon, a name he borrowed from the Suisun Indians.

Napa Valley, with microclimatic conditions ideal for grape growing, has been called an agricultural preserve. Over twenty-two thousand acres are under cultivation here. Highway 29, running through Yountville, Oakville, Rutherford, and St. Helena, is the hotline of the Napa wineries. A parallel road, the Silverado Trail, is a more leisurely route, high enough for panoramic views of the vineyards. The two roads meet at various crossroads, so you can zigzag back and forth to visit the wineries of your choice.

Roving the Napa Valley turns up some interests extracurricular to enology. One of the world's three regularly erupting geysers, California's own Old Faithful, shows off every fifty minutes just north of Calistoga. The town itself is famous as a health resort of hot springs and mud baths. Fans of Robert Louis Stevenson can haunt the Silverado Mine near St. Helena to look for ghosts.

The southwestern end of the Russian River, especially near Guerneville, is a river playground. Cruising down the river—in inner tubes, rafts, or canoes—is favorite family fun in the summertime. In fall and winter it's the scene of serious fishing.

Northwest of Cloverdale, the Navarro River flows to the sea through the

Anderson Valley, a fifteen-mile stretch where the wineries are within shouting distance of one another along Highway 128. The Anderson Valley is also known as apple country. One orchard alone produces thirty different varieties. Historical Boonville is a treat, whether or not you harp (speak) Boontling, the imaginative dialect spoken by the Boonters who live here.

Many people think of boating, fishing, and water skiing when you mention Clear Lake, but wine lovers will be glad to know that a re-emergence of Lake County wineries is well under way. In the early 1900's, more than thirty Lake County wineries produced wine that won gold medals in American and European competitions. The difficulty of shipping wine over the rugged mountains that surround the county, and then Prohibition, caused most of the wineries to die on the vine. Today these are no longer problems, and several important wineries flourish here to tempt travelers. And of course, there still is the attraction of Clear Lake, the largest natural lake within California's borders (Lake Tahoe is bigger, but we share it with Nevada), the perfect place to picnic and dream up some additions to Kazantzakis's list.

Big Yellow Sunflower   **(707) 965-3885**
235 Sky Oaks Drive, Angwin, CA 94508
(Above Napa Valley—east side)

The Big Yellow Sunflower is a private apartment suite adjacent to the home of Betty and Dale Clement. It is situated near Angwin in a lush little valley on top of Howell Mountain, a gorgeous ten-minute drive from the Napa Valley. Decorated in golds and browns, the spacious suite includes a living area with a large fireplace as its focal point, a kitchenette, bath, loft bedroom, and private deck. Besides the total comfort and seclusion, the specialty at this B&B is home grown and prepared foods. Walnut trees, a grape arbor, and a garden just outside the back door yield a bountiful array of items that are served to guests. Imported cheeses, fresh fruits, homemade cookies, and Häagen-Dazs ice cream are complimentary on arrival. The suite is a wonderful hideaway retreat where you may do nothing more strenuous than relax and catch up on your reading, or you may find refuge after an exciting day in the Napa Valley. A gracious welcome is yours at the sign of the Big Yellow Sunflower.

No pets or smoking; children welcome; large brunch; homemade vegetable soup in the evening for $1; TV; kitchenette; up to five adults can be accommodated; airport pickup (Angwin).

Room	Bed	Bath	Entrance	Floor	Daily Rates S - D	(EP)
A	2Q	Pvt	Sep	1G	$55-$65	($10)

Colfax's Guest House   **(707) 895-3241**
Box 246, Boonville, CA 95415
(Above the Anderson Valley)

I have found another reason for visiting the Anderson Valley besides the New Boonville Hotel Restaurant, noteworthy up-and-coming wineries, gorgeous countryside, and proximity to the Mendocino coast: Colfax's Guest House. The Colfaxes are extraordinary people indeed, and you may even have heard of them—they educated their children at home, and the eldest son attends Harvard. Resourceful and talented, they built the self-contained guest house on their working ranch from redwoods felled and hand-milled on the property. The bedroom, bath, kitchen area, and living room with woodstove are masterfully constructed and finished to the last detail. The natural simplicity of the decor enhances the collection of original artwork on the walls. The silence and fresh air, the majesty of redwoods, and glimpses of the valley below add up to an unforgettable setting for a special getaway.

Children welcome; full breakfast on weekends; two futons in living room. **KNIGHTTIME PUBLICATIONS SPECIAL RATE: $50 Sunday-Thursday nights with this book.

Room	Bed	Bath	Entrance	Floor	Daily Rates S - D	(EP)
A	1Q	Pvt	Sep	1	$75	($10)

Foothill House   **(707) 942-6933**
3037 Foothill Boulevard, Calistoga, CA 94515
(Western foothills just north of Calistoga)

Foothill House is definitely *special.* Gnarled old trees, abundant wild-life, and sweeping views across the valley characterize the setting. Formerly a simple farmhouse, the home has been remodeled in first-rate fashion. Guest rooms are spacious and individually decorated with country antiques. The color scheme in each room is derived from the handmade quilt that covers the four-poster bed. Hosts Michael and Susan Clow offer every amenity to pamper and please their guests. A wine-appreciation hour is held in the late afternoon, and a generous Continental breakfast is served in the morning. Each can be a social or private occasion, depending on whether you partake in the sunroom, on the terrace, or in your room. The Clows' concern for each guest is genuine, the quality of their lodgings superior. You don't have to wait for a special event to go to Foothill House—just being there is reason enough to celebrate.

No pets or smoking; well-behaved child over twelve welcome (one per room in A and C); AC, ceiling fan, fireplace, and refrigerator in each room; sleeper sofa in Room A; alcove bed in C. Brochure available. $5 midweek discount November-April.

Room	Bed	Bath	Entrance	Floor	Daily Rates S - D	(EP)
A	1Q	Pvt	Sep	1	$80	($15)
B	1Q	Pvt	Sep	1	$75	
C	1T & 1Q	Pvt	Sep	1	$100	($15)

House of a Thousand Flowers   **(707) 632-5571**
P.O. Box 369, Monte Rio, CA 95462
(Five miles east of Jenner-by-the-Sea)

When you arrive at the House of a Thousand Flowers, you know right away how it got its name. Greenery, including fuchsias and other blossoming plants, bedeck the house and infuse it with cheer. Hosts Jan and Dave Silva take pride in the family home that is now a remote country haven for harried city folk in need of escape. The house is set high on a bluff above the Russian River and has two cozy guest rooms on its lower level. Each has its own deck, separate entrance, and access to an enclosed, plant-filled spa. Look toward the sea and you may witness the magical effect created as fingers of fog move through the redwoods. The main floor is also yours to enjoy, with grand piano, extensive library, and dining room where Chef David serves his famous omelettes. Coffee is ready by your room when you wake up, and breakfast is served at your convenience anytime during the morning. Discover a little slice of paradise at the House of a Thousand Flowers.

Dog and cat in residence; full breakfast; afternoon refreshments; rollaway bed available; spa; river and ocean activities, good restaurants and wineries nearby. Brochure available.

Room	Bed	Bath	Entrance	Floor	Daily Rates S - D	(EP)
A	1Q	Shd*	Sep	LL	$65	($10)
B	1Q	Shd*	Sep	LL	$65	($10)

Robert & Ingrid Hansen   **(707) 994-7313**
5128 Swedberg Road, Lower Lake, CA 95457
(Baylis Point)

    Robert Hansen built this charming Bavarian cottage—which manages to be quaint without being cute—some years ago, and it's a delight just to look at. There's moss growing on the roof, an ancient gnarled tree by the front door, stained-glass windows, and a quiet lakefront setting. Inside, beautifully carved, aged wood and a large, stone fireplace create an impression of glowing warmth. Guests occupy the home's upper level, consisting of two bedrooms, a sitting area, and a bath. Guest rooms are small and immaculate, with comforters on the beds and a cozy, European ambiance. Though most people visit during warm weather to enjoy the lake's activities, I think staying overnight at the Hansens' would be a joy any time of year.

    Cat in residence; no pets or children; no smoking in bedrooms; full breakfast; TV; AC; sitting area upstairs; kitchen privileges by arrangement; deck; barbecue; private beach; dock; seaplane landing; skiing; windsurfing; golf, tennis, horseback riding, and dining nearby; German, Spanish, French, and Italian spoken; airport pickup (Pierce, Santa Rosa). Room B available only for two parties traveling together. Reduced rates after three days.

Room	Bed	Bath	Entrance	Floor	Daily Rates S - D	(EP)
A	1D	Pvt	Main	2	$35-$45	
B	1D		Main	2	$35-$45	

Muktip Manor   **(707) 994-9571**
12540 Lakeshore Drive, Clearlake, CA 95422
(South shore of lake)

The home of Elisabeth St. Davids and Jerry Schiffman (affectionately known as Muktip Manor) has a peculiar, Early California charm of its own. The living quarters are all on the second floor, with doors opening onto a wrap-around veranda. Located opposite the lake, it affords good views and a small, private beach. The guest unit consists of a bedroom, living room, kitchen, and bath. While far from luxurious, the decor is delightfully eclectic. Elisabeth is a journalist, and Jerry, a former actor. (Look for him on reruns of *Streets of San Francisco*; Elisabeth says, "He always played a cop or a corpse.") They enjoy sailing their catamaran most every evening. Whatever your particular pleasure might be, there's a host of activities to choose from: boating, windsurfing, swimming, canoeing, fishing, rock-hunting, and wine-tasting at Lake County wineries. The lifestyle at Muktip Manor is casual, unpretentious, and laced with humor—a thoroughly engaging combination.

Two dogs and many cats in residence; no children; full breakfast; TV; kitchen; large deck; launch ramp and public fishing piers nearby; extra meals optional; French, German, and Spanish spoken; airport pickup (Pierce). Animal lovers preferred.

Room	Bed	Bath	Entrance	Floor	Daily Rates S - D	(EP)
A	1D	Pvt	Sep	2	$30-$40	($10)

The Campbell Ranch   **(707) 857-3476**
1475 Canyon Road, Geyserville, CA 95441
(Two miles west of U.S. 101)

Mary Jane and Jerry Campbell's hillside home offers spectacular views of the rolling vineyards of Sonoma County. Guests may play tennis, horseshoes, or Ping-Pong and go hiking or swimming without even leaving the ranch. Located close by are Sonoma County wineries, Warm Springs Dam and Lake Sonoma, a fish hatchery, geysers, a network of bike trails, and excellent restaurants. The Campbells provide a luxurious array of elegant touches to make your stay special: lavish breakfasts are served on the terrace; fresh flowers, fruit, and wine are in each room; lemonade and iced tea are served poolside and courtside; pie and coffee may be enjoyed before retiring. When you visit The Campbell Ranch, bring your camera, your tennis racket, and an appetite for Mary Jane's delicious cooking.

No pets or children; smoking outside only; full breakfast; AC; TV in Room A; queen sofa bed in C; patio; swimming pool; tennis court; airport pickup at extra charge (Santa Rosa-Sonoma County, Cloverdale, Healdsburg). Two-night minimum on weekends.

Room	Bed	Bath	Entrance	Floor	Daily Rates S - D	(EP)
A	1K	Pvt	Sep	1G	$80	
B	1K	Shd*	Main	2	$80	
C	1K	Shd*	Main	2	$80	($25)

Santa Nella House   **(707) 869-9488**
12130 Highway 116, Guerneville, CA 95446
(Seventeen miles east of Jenner-by-the-Sea)

Santa Nella House is steeped in the history of the Russian River area. It rests on the site of the first olive mill and lumber mill and was the main dwelling of the Santa Nella Winery (established 1880). Nestled among old redwoods, the house is a white country Victorian with a wide, wrap-around porch. High ceilings, deep red carpeting, and lovely turn-of-the-century furnishings make an elegant impression. Each guest room is special in its own way, and choosing among them isn't easy. Some very efficient woodstoves keep the house thoroughly toasty. The abundant hospitality of hosts Ed and Joyce Ferrington includes a sampling of local wines and hors d'oeuvres, a generous champagne brunch, and a soak in the large redwood hot tub on the side porch. The Russian River area offers numerous outdoor activities, notable wineries, and excellent restaurants. The Ferringtons are more than happy to help you sort them all out. At Santa Nella House, you will be comfortable and well taken care of.

Dog and cat in residence; no pets or smoking; teenagers welcome; champagne brunch; TV; library; hot tub; fireplace in Room A; airport pickup (Santa Rosa, Sonoma County).

Room	Bed	Bath	Entrance	Floor	Daily Rates S - D	(EP)
A	1D	Pvt	Main	1	$60	
B	1D	Pvt	Main	1	$60	
C	1T & 1D	Shd*	Main	2	$60	($15)
D	1D	Shd*	Main	2	$60	

Gee-Gee's   **(707) 833-6667**
7810 Sonoma Highway, Santa Rosa, CA 95405
(On Highway 12 in the Valley of the Moon)

Gerda Heaton-Weisz has been offering quality lodgings to travelers for many years. In 1981, she moved Gee-Gee's of Quincy from the Feather River country to the wine country. (Three wineries are within a mile of Gee-Gee's.) Four pleasant guest rooms are available for bed and breakfast, two in the main house and two in a separate guest cottage. The swimming pool can surely look inviting after an arduous day on the road. Gerda attended the Sorbonne and speaks French fluently. She brings some of her European traditions to the hospitality she provides. What she appreciates most about her present setting is the "view of mountains on three sides, cattle grazing across the road, and seemingly endless stretches of prune and walnut trees bordering my one acre...." I, for one, am glad she decided to share it.

Dog and cat in residence; no pets, children, or smoking; full breakfast served on deck or in dining room; sitting room with fireplace and TV; decks; swimming pool; bicycles; hiking and jogging trails, horseback riding, and golfing nearby; French and German spoken; airport connections by arrangement (Santa Rosa). Rooms A and B share a bath; C and D share a bath. 20% off-season discount to AARP members; 10% rest of year. **KNIGHTTIME PUBLICATIONS SPECIAL RATE: 10% discount with this book.

Room	Bed	Bath	Entrance	Floor	Daily Rates S - D	(EP)
A	1D	Shd*	Main	1G	$40-$50	($20)
B	1D	Shd*	Main	1G	$40-$50	($20)
C	1Q	Shd*	Sep	1G	$55	($20)
D	2T	Shd*	Sep	1G	$55	($20)

Gallery Osgood   **(707) 224-0100**
2230 First Street, Napa, CA 94559
(Two blocks east of Highway 29)

Bed and breakfast in an art gallery? I liked the idea, but I didn't know how much until I toured this splendidly restored Queen Anne home. Professional artists Joan Osgood and Howard Moehrke live and work on the premises. This exceptional husband and wife team have between them all the talents necessary to make the unique concept work. Perhaps only artists can decorate with such a flourish, create such lavish breakfasts, and arrange the gallery space to such advantage. Their work, as well as that of other award-winning artists, is on display. Eleven-foot ceilings and bay windows give the home a light, airy look. B&B visitors stay in three elegant guest rooms with a shared bath. The comfortable living room is a fine place to relax, and the exquisitely landscaped yard invites a stroll. If I had to sum up the Gallery Osgood in just one word, I think I could—perfection.

Dog and cat in residence; no pets. For more details about the guest rooms, the decor, your hosts, and the art gallery, write *early* for a brochure— many others have discovered this B&B!

Room	Bed	Bath	Entrance	Floor	Daily Rates S - D	(EP)
A	1D	Shd*	Main	1	$70	
B	1Q	Shd*	Main	1	$70	
C	1Q	Shd*	Main	1	$70	

Bylund House (707) 963-9073
2000 Howell Mountain Road, St. Helena, CA 94574 or 963-1307
(Two miles east of Silverado Trail)

The Bylunds' striking new home is set in a quiet, secluded spot just minutes from major wineries and other attractions of the Napa Valley. The large pink stucco house surrounded by rolling hills is reminiscent of a villa in the Italian countryside. The guest tower has a separate entrance and consists of a parlor with bar and refrigerator, and a bedroom and bath on each of two floors above. The decor has a clean, cool, natural look that I found refreshing and elegant. There are custom bedcoverings, high poster beds, and pine armoires. Relax on one of the balconies and bask in the peaceful atmosphere. Bylund B&B is a romantic place to slow down and renew your energies amid the many indulgences that are part of a wine country getaway.

No pets, children, or smoking; AC; lap pool; two-night minimum on weekends. Brochure available. **KNIGHTTIME PUBLICATIONS SPECIAL RATE: $10 less midweek November-April, except holidays, with this book.

Room	Bed	Bath	Entrance	Floor	Daily Rates S - D	(EP)
A	1Q	Pvt	Sep	2	$75	
B	1Q	Pvt	Sep	3	$75	

Deer Run Bed & Breakfast   (707) 963-3794
3995 Spring Mountain Road, St. Helena, CA 94574
(Five miles west of Highway 29, above the Napa Valley)

As you wind your way along the road up Spring Mountain, glancing back occasionally for views of the valley below, the anticipation begins to build. Once you reach Deer Run, you will be well rewarded. It's a rustic gem of a home on four acres belonging to Tom and Carol Wilson. There are two guest units, each with a private bath and entrance, one with a fireplace (B). The swimming pool looks enticing, and the deck is a great place to relax among the trees. You may even see some deer, for the property really *is* a deer run. You can enjoy this private hideaway in its tranquil, secluded setting and still be only minutes from shops, restaurants, spas, and the wineries for which the valley is famous. Spring Mountain itself (Tom's birthplace) boasts a number of wineries that give special consideration to Deer Run's guests. In every respect, the Wilsons aim to provide top-notch hospitality.

Dog and three cats in residence; no pets or children; no smoking preferred; complimentary sherry and TV in each room; swimming pool.

Room	Bed	Bath	Entrance	Floor	Daily Rates S - D	(EP)
A	1Q	Pvt	Sep	1	$61	
B	1K	Pvt	Sep	1	$71	

Judy's Bed & Breakfast   (707) 963-3081
2036 Madrona Avenue, St. Helena, CA 94574
(One-half mile west of Main Street—Highway 29)

You'll get a warm, wine-country welcome at Judy's. Bob and Judy
Sculatti have lived on their nine-acre vineyard for many years. They've converted a spacious, private room at one end of their home to a B&B accommodation of great charm and comfort. The large space is furnished with lovely
antiques, Oriental rugs, and a romantic brass bed. Complimentary wine and
cheese are served upon your arrival. After a day of touring and tasting, or even
a hot-air balloon ride, you can come back to Judy's for a refreshing dip in the
pool. To round out your perfect day, dine at one of the Napa Valley's superb
restaurants.

No pets, children, or RV parking; no smoking preferred; TV; AC; swimming pool; sauna; barbecue; Italian spoken. Brochure available. $10 extra
charge for Saturday night only; 10% midweek discount.

Room	Bed	Bath	Entrance	Floor	Daily Rates S - D	(EP)
A	1Q	Pvt	Sep	1G	$65	

Judy's Ranch House   **(707) 963-3081**
701 Rossi Road, St. Helena, CA 94574
(Just west of Silverado Trail in Conn Valley)

The Sculatti family now operates an additional B&B home on the opposite side of the Napa Valley but just as accessible to it. The spacious, comfortable ranch-style home is built around an interior courtyard. Everywhere you look, there are idyllic views of the Conn Valley countryside. Guests have use of an inviting living room with fireplace, a large country kitchen, and a Jacuzzi spa—a marvelous place to unwind while watching cattle, deer, and quail feed in neighboring pastures and vineyards. You're also welcome to relax with a glass of wine on the front porch, which looks out upon century-old oak trees lining a seasonal creek. Each bedroom has a ceiling fan, private bath, and hillside view. The Sculattis can help you with plans for enjoying the Napa Valley's many attractions.

No pets; smoking outside only; complimentary wine; Jacuzzi spa. Brochure available. $10 extra charge for Saturday night only; 10% midweek discount.

Room	Bed	Bath	Entrance	Floor	Daily Rates S - D	(EP)
A	2T or 1K	Pvt	Main	1G	$75	
B	1Q	Pvt	Main	1G	$75	

Helga Poulsen   **(707) 758-1661**
P.O. Box 3211, Santa Rosa, CA 95403
(Northeastern Santa Rosa)

The Poulsens' striking, new contemporary home is set high on a hill among large oak trees, commanding sweeping views of Santa Rosa and beautiful wine country scenery. It has high, vaulted ceilings, stone fireplaces, and big, round decks. There is a great feeling of spaciousness throughout the house, and you'll have a choice of places to relax. Although the Poulsens' home is only minutes from downtown, it seems remote from the rest of the world. A native Britisher, Helga offers guests the traditional hospitality of her homeland. She can recommend some worthwhile spots to visit in the Santa Rosa-Sonoma area. Helga also operates "Wine Country Bed & Breakfast," a referral service that lists a number of homes, in addition to hers, offering B&B lodging. Give her a call and let her help you find just the accommodations you're looking for.

No pets, children, or smoking; full breakfast; sitting room with TV; German and some French spoken.

Room	Bed	Bath	Entrance	Floor	Daily Rates S - D	(EP)
A	2T	Shd*	Main	LL	$40-$55	

Alene Maches   **(707) 996-7178**
18860 Melvin Avenue, Sonoma, CA 95476
(Off Highway 12 in the Valley of the Moon)

You'll be warmly received in the home of Alene Maches. It's located in a quiet, secure neighborhood on the northern edge of Sonoma. Two of her three tidy bedrooms are used for B&B guests. Breakfast is served in the large, sunny kitchen. Through the window, you can view the well-tended yard where flowers and fruit trees display their seasonal bounty. When staying at Mrs. Maches's home, you'll be only a short distance from the Valley of the Moon, the Plaza in Sonoma, and an interesting mix of historical and enological attractions unique to this part of Sonoma County. If you do a little research in advance, you're sure to make some intriguing discoveries.

Children welcome; TV; kitchen privileges; patio and garden; barbecue.

Room	Bed	Bath	Entrance	Floor	Daily Rates S - D	(EP)
A	1D	Shd	Main	1G	$25	
B	1T	Shd	Main	1G	$20	

Redwood House   **(707) 895-3526**
21340 Highway 128, Yorkville, CA 95494
(Twenty miles from Cloverdale and U.S. 101)

I call Redwood House a buried treasure. It's tucked into the woods in a part of the wine country which is only just being discovered—a real "find." Leslie and Freda Hanelt have a private guest cottage that's all redwood and glass. It has a living room with a woodstove, a kitchenette, a bath, and a spiral staircase leading to a sleeping loft. The views from within are of trees, sky, and a creek you can swim or row in during the summer. There are wooded paths to explore, a small children's beach, and two decks overlooking the creek. The Hanelts take pleasure in sharing this heavenly spot with their guests, whose options include wine-tasting at fine Anderson Valley wineries, side-tripping to the Mendocino coast (thirty-five miles away), or simply settling into the freedom and joy of country living. An added bonus: works of culinary genius are produced at the nearby New Boonville Hotel.

Children welcome; no smoking preferred; sofa bed and crib available; sauna; playhouse; German and Greek spoken. Two-night minimum.

Room	Bed	Bath	Entrance	Floor	Daily Rates S - D	(EP)
A	1T & 1D	Pvt	Sep	2	$35-$40	($10)

The use of travelling is to regu-

late imagination by reality, and

instead of thinking how things

may be, to see them as they

are.

—Samuel Johnson

A guest never forgets the host

who has treated him kindly.

—Homer

Central
Valley
to
Mount
Shasta

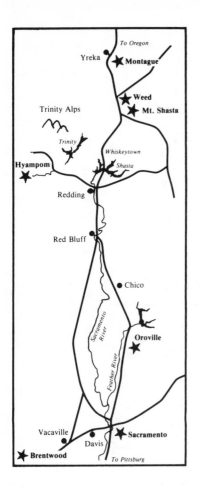

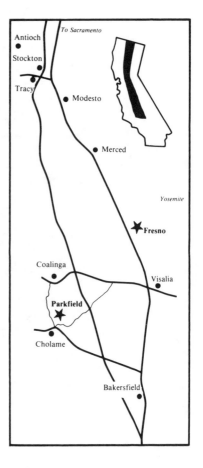

CENTRAL VALLEY TO MOUNT SHASTA

California's Central Valley is the richest, most varied agricultural area in the nation. Everything from fruit to nuts, literally, is grown here; two hundred forty different farm products are cultivated within these nineteen counties.

What this means for the traveler is that Highway 5 need not be boring. Although designed for people on their way to Somewhere Else, Highway 5 (and parallel 99) has many treats in store for the curious traveler, the kind of person who wants to know what a kiwi vine looks like. Many of the farms near the highways are open for tours and pick-it-yourself purists. Farmers' markets and stands do a brisk business. There are good picnic spots, too. For example, the area around Merced boasts three state parks, offering swimming and fishing, as well as cool oases to sample those melons you bought in Kings County and that dessert wine from Fresno.

The Central Valley is really two valleys. The southern valley is drained by the San Joaquin River, and the northern one is drained by the Sacramento. The two rivers meet in one of California's nicest surprises, the delightful Delta. The Delta is a rough, seven hundred forty thousand-acre triangle with Pittsburg at its western point, Sacramento its northern, and Tracy its southern. About eleven hundred miles of levees rim fifty-five islands reclaimed from marshland. Disappointment Slough, Bacon Island, Little Potato—the place names alone are worth the trip.

New visitors may be startled to see freighters sedately plowing through fields of waving grain. Actually, the ships are in the water where they belong, hidden to the gunwales by the levees. You can drive along the levees, crossing from one bank to another on cantilevered drawbridges. Tiny Delta towns like Locke (an old Chinese community under consideration as an historical park) and Clarksburg date back to steamboat days. Boating (including houseboats) and fishing are big business here.

At the northern tip of the Delta is Sacramento. In 1849, Sacramento was the gateway to the Gold Rush, and a visit to restored "Old Sac" brings back the days of prospectors, plank sidewalks, and the Pony Express. A bronze rider is a monument to the boys who answered the following ad: *Wanted— Young, skinny, wiry fellows not over eighteen. Must be expert riders, willing to risk death daily. Orphans preferred.*

Sutter's Fort, which predates Sacramento by about ten years, and the State Indian Museum, which predates Sutter's Fort by many more, are other historical highlights, as is the Railroad Museum. The newly restored State Capitol building is a living work of art well worth a visit. So is the renovated Governor's Mansion, which today is free of the rats and bats that former residents complained of. A pleasant alternative to pounding the path of history is to bike along the American River Parkway, which has picnic tables, restrooms, and other facilities.

North of Sacramento lies the Feather River country with fern-filled canyons, pine-covered mountains, and chaparral slopes. The river was dubbed by Don Luis Arguello, who happened to be out exploring during a migration of band-tailed pigeons that filled the river with feathers.

Oroville, in the center of the Feather River region, is rich in history.

California's largest Chinatown flourished here in the 1870's, and the four-structure Chinese Temple still stands. Another landmark is the Lott home, a gothic revival-style Victorian, surrounded by Sank Park. With a great deal of grace and charm, the park's regularity and symmetry were designed to express "the taste and affluence of the successful Victorian businessman."

Nearby is Lake Oroville, the site of the highest dam in the United States and a profusion of aquatic activity. A little farther east is Feather Falls, a picturesque cascade plunging six hundred forty feet. To the north is the famed Feather River Canyon, one of the most beautiful in California and a favorite for trout fishing.

Redding marks the beginning of California's water wonderland. The Big Three—Whiskeytown, Shasta, and Trinity (Clair Engle) Lakes—make up a paradise for boaters, anglers, swimmers, water skiers, sailors, and windsurfers. To the east, Burney Falls drops a gossamer curtain of water at a rate of twenty-three hundred gallons per second. Fragrant cedar, fir, oak, willow, and cottonwood maintain the cool on even the hottest summer day.

Rivers, creeks, and streams abound throughout the area, and there are many smaller lakes as well. One stunner is Lake Siskiyou, a natural mirror for Mount Shasta's majestic profile. Nearby, glacier-polished Castle Crags rear up six thousand feet.

Just getting to the Shasta Caverns is an interesting trip. A catamaran cruise across an arm of Lake Shasta and a dizzying bus ride up a steep mountainside bring you to the cave entrance. Inside are magical limestone columns, draperies, and formations that look like soda straws or peanut brittle or spaghetti or. . .well, most visitors like to come up with their own comparisons.

The Mount Shasta area would be an idyllic destination for a highway, but Highway 5 does not stop here. It continues on into Oregon and beyond. But that, of course, is Somewhere Else.

Diablo Vista   **(415) 634-2396**
Route 2, Box 221B, Brentwood, CA 94513
(Just east of Antioch, off Lone Tree Way)

This elegant ranch-style home is set on two acres of fruit and nut trees, with a view of Mount Diablo in the distance. It is an hour from San Francisco and just ten minutes from the Sacramento River Delta, known far and wide as a boating and fishing mecca. Brentwood, four miles away, is famous for the many "U-Pick" fruit and vegetable farms around it. Maps showing the various farms and their offerings are easily obtainable. The guest room at Diablo Vista is located at its far end, well separated from the rest of the house. The huge space has its own entrance, bath, kitchenette, small library, TV, and stereo system. A harmonious, soothing effect is created by the use of subtle colors, Oriental rugs, and custom-made futons and window cushions. Guests are welcome to swim in the pool, soak in the hot tub, or sip a drink in the gazebo. Hosts Dick and Myra Hackett have thoroughly searched out the best restaurants in the area, a boon to those of us who take our dining seriously.

No pets; children over eight (swimmers) welcome; smoking outside only; TV and stereo; kitchenette; swimming pool and hot tub; jogging and biking trails surround property; some Spanish spoken; airport pickup (Antioch).

Room	Bed	Bath	Entrance	Floor	Daily Rates S - D	(EP)
A	2D	Pvt	Sep	1G	$45-$50	

The Country Victorian   **(209) 233-1988**
1003 South Orange Avenue, Fresno, CA 93702
(Southeast downtown area)

When the Robinson family built this home in 1900, it was a country farmhouse located outside the city limits. A residential neighborhood has since grown up around it. Howard and Nancy English are only the second owners of the home, and they feel a strong connection to its past. When they bought it in 1977, it still held many of the original family's belongings. Photos, furnishings, and mementos can be seen throughout the interior, and Nancy has added many collections of her own. Some newer touches have made the home more comfortable, but nostalgia remains the key ingredient. Two accommodations serve B&B guests—an upstairs room with lots of charm, and a luxurious suite on the main floor. The suite connects to an atrium containing a hot tub and an aviary. Your hosts are long-time residents; they can guide you to historic home tours and help you choose among Fresno's diverse and plentiful restaurants.

Birds in aviary; no pets; smoking outside only; TV; extra guests use queen sofa bed in suite (B); hot tub; many lakes in area around Fresno; Kings Canyon and Sequoia National Parks, one hour away; Yosemite, two hours.

Room	Bed	Bath	Entrance	Floor	Daily Rates S - D	(EP)
A	1D	Shd	Main	2	$30-$35	
B	1Q	Pvt	Sep	1	$40-$45	($5)

The Areys   **(916) 628-5953**
P.O. Box 1, Hyampom, CA 96046
(Shasta-Trinity Wilderness Area, between Redding and Eureka)

Hyampom is, to date, the most remote location in this book. Imagine how pleased I was, after two hours on winding mountain roads, to find a bucolic little valley where life goes on largely untouched by the outside world. It was a rare experience, and I reveled in it. Honey and Joe Arey are long-time residents of Hyampom and thoroughly delightful people. They have a guest apartment, separate from the main house, that is very comfortable and blessed with a view I could stare at for hours: an apple orchard, a green pasture with grazing sheep, a prolific vegetable garden, and a backdrop of beautiful mountains. For anyone seeking to escape the distractions of the modern world for a while, The Areys is a perfect destination. The only problem is, you may not want to leave.

Outdoor animals on property; no pets; smoking outside only; choice of full or Continental breakfast; TV; kitchen; double sofa bed in living room; fishing, swimming, hiking, cookouts, and birdwatching in area; airport pickup (Hyampom).

Room	Bed	Bath	Entrance	Floor	Daily Rates S - D	(EP)
A	1D	Pvt	Sep	1	$35	($10)

Greenleaf Ranch   **(916) 628-5558**
P.O. Box 166, Hyampom, CA 96046
(Shasta-Trinity Wilderness Area, between Redding and Eureka)

Sandy and Mark Greenleaf have a working cattle ranch on the site of an 1854 homestead (with the original log home still standing) near the tiny village of Hyampom. There are two rustic, private cottages for B&B guests. Sandy's special touches have made them cozy and charming. The peacefulness and beauty of the surroundings will astonish city dwellers. The Greenleafs provide a delicious full breakfast, afternoon tea, arrangements for dinner at a local cafe, and guidance to the nearby river for swimming and fishing. Private pilots are treated to unique limousine service (be surprised). Remote as it may be, Greenleaf Ranch is worth going out of your way for.

Full breakfast and afternoon tea; hunting (guides available for bear and deer), fishing, and swimming nearby; airport pickup (Hyampom). Ranch located on same road as The Areys.

Room	Bed	Bath	Entrance	Floor	Daily Rates S - D	(EP)
A	1T & 1D	Pvt	Sep	1	$30-$40	($10)
B	1D	Pvt	Sep	1	$30-$40	

Julian Beaudroit House, 1903   **(916) 459-5449**
P.O. Box 746, Montague, CA 96064
(Seven miles east of Yreka at I-5)

Chet and Dora Shelden have put down roots in the picturesque Shasta Valley where Chet holds a teaching post in a one-room country schoolhouse. He and Dora bought a historic Victorian home in the tiny town of Montague in 1983 and have worked hard to restore it to the restrained elegance of its heyday. The home has stained-glass windows, a clawfoot bathtub, and much of its original charm. A pretty bedroom with a bay window and garden view is the main guest room, with an additional room upstairs. For your pleasure, there is a sun room with TV and library, and a deck by the beautiful rose garden. A stop at the Julian Beaudroit House takes you off the hurried corridor of I-5 and beckons you to just slow down. You'll find back roads to explore, stunning views of Mount Shasta, and fine mountain and lake recreation nearby. The Ashland Shakespeare Festival is forty-five minutes away and the Klamath River, about thirty. An all-day excursion to Lava Beds National Monument is a one-of-a-kind thrill.

No pets; smoking outside only; older children by arrangement; some Spanish spoken; airport pickup (Montague).

Room	Bed	Bath	Entrance	Floor	Daily Rates S - D	(EP)
A	1D	Shd	Main	1	$30-$35	($10)
B	2T	Shd	Main	2	$30-$35	

Ward's "Big Foot" Ranch   **(916) 926-5170**
P.O. Box 585, Mount Shasta, CA 96067
(1530 Hill Road; two miles northwest of I-5)

Barbara and Phil Ward, formerly educators from Saratoga, have realized a dream in returning to Phil's native Mount Shasta to live. Their rural ranch-style home is situated for maximum views of the splendid mammoth mountain. The huge, wrap-around deck and most of the rooms are outstanding viewing spots. Inside and out, the home is beautifully maintained. It has the feeling of a luxury resort with homey touches. Guest rooms have special comfort and charm. The Wards are fond of entertaining and cooking for guests. (Phil's delicious *aebleskivers*, usually served on weekends, have become a tradition.) On starry nights, gazing through a telescope from the deck is a sparkling experience. A restful atmosphere and unprecedented views of Mount Shasta are yours at Ward's "Big Foot" Ranch.

Outdoor pets include dog, burro, geese, and peacocks; no pets (indoors); full breakfast; refreshments; TV; living room for guests; kitchen privileges by arrangement; barbecue; tours by school bus; trout stream on property; hiking trails nearby; horseshoes, Ping-Pong, and croquet in summer; downhill and Nordic ski areas nearby; bus, train, or airport (Dunsmuir, Weed) pickup. Sofa bed in family room available at $30 a night; extra-long twin beds that convert to a king in Room B. **KNIGHTTIME PUBLICATIONS SPECIAL RATE: 10% discount with this book.

Room	Bed	Bath	Entrance	Floor	Daily Rates S - D	(EP)
A	1D	Shd*	Main	1	$35-$40	
B	2T or 1K	Shd*	Main	1	$35-$40	

Jean's Riverside Bed & Breakfast   **(916) 533-1413**
P.O. Box 2334, Oroville, CA 95965
(1124 Middlehoff Lane)

     Jean Pratt's rustic home is set on the west bank of the Feather River. Sliding glass doors open to a deck and a lawn that slopes gently to the waterfront. Lucky visitors are treated to idyllic views of the river and peaceful countryside, as well as easy access to swimming, boating, fishing, and panning for gold. Jean's acreage is so spacious and still that it's a haven for friendly wildlife. Your host, a seasoned traveler herself, knows an amazing variety of places in the area to explore. She recommends Feather Falls, Table Mountain, the Chinese Temple, the Pioneer Museum, historic cemeteries, and the Oroville Dam and Fish Hatchery (with up-to-date facilities, especially interesting during salmon run; personal tours arranged with advance notice). Oroville and the surrounding area are rich in culture, history, recreation, and scenery.

     No pets (indoors); TVs and canoes available; extra charge for children, airport pickup, laundry and cooking facilities; host suggests day trips from Oroville to Sacramento, Grass Valley, Lake Tahoe, Mount Lassen, and Mount Shasta. Phone device answered after caller gives name and phone number; if not answered, also give address and reservation dates. Private suite with 1D & 1Q also available, rates from $50 to $80; any room available with private bath, $5 extra.

Room	Bed	Bath	Entrance	Floor	Daily Rates S - D	(EP)
A	1T & 1D	Shd*	Sep	1G	$25-$35	
B	2T	Shd*	Sep	1G	$25-$35	
C	1D	Pvt	Sep	1G	$35-$40	
D	1Q	Shd*	Sep	1G	$35-$40	
E	1K	Shd*	Sep	1G	$45	

Martin & Gloria Van Horn   **(805) 463-2320**
R.R. Box 3625, San Miguel, CA 93451
(Between U.S. 101 and I-5, twelve miles north of Cholame & Hwy 46)

This eight-hundred-acre ranch in the Cholame Valley is the homestead where the Van Horns have lived all their lives. Though it is remote, finding their property is easy. It gives you a chance to get off the major highways and onto some of the loveliest back roads in California. The rambling modern ranch house has a living room with a massive stone fireplace. Three commodious guest rooms have a rustic ranch look. Outside, the wide open spaces are yours to roam at will. Horses graze in the fields, birds soar above, and wildflowers abound. Hiking along a creek in the clean, fresh air is sure to put some color in your cheeks. Take a swim or soak in the Jacuzzi, catch up on your reading, visit some local wineries; extraordinary peace and quiet await you at the Van Horns' ranch.

Dogs, cats, horses, and cows on ranch; no pets or children; no smoking in bedrooms; swimming pool; spa. Ask about deluxe ranch plan.

Room	Bed	Bath	Entrance	Floor	Daily Rates S - D	(EP)
A	1Q	Shd*	Main	1G	$45	
B	1D	Shd*	Main	1G	$40	
C	1K	Pvt	Main	1G	$55	

Vera J. Wallner   **(916) 455-1392**
4308 G Street, Sacramento, CA 95819
(East Sacramento)

   The private guest cottage behind Mrs. Wallner's home overlooks a patio garden scene that is as pretty as a photo in *Sunset* magazine. Such a quiet, secluded setting can be hard to find in a metropolitan area like Sacramento. What an enchanting spot for this complete, small-scale home away from home. Many travelers find it perfectly suited to their needs. Mrs. Wallner sometimes serves her guests tea from a musical teapot, one of her handpainted creations. While visiting California's capital, you'll enjoy the security and convenience of her lovely, older neighborhood.

   No pets, children, smoking, or drinking; full breakfast; TV; kitchenette; bus service; airport pickup (Executive, or Metropolitan for $5).

Room	Bed	Bath	Entrance	Floor	Daily Rates S - D	(EP)
A	2T	Pvt	Sep	1G	$25-$30	

Barbiers' Bed & Breakfast **(916) 938-3359**
5843 Floyd Court, Weed, CA 96094
(Between I-5 and Highway 97)

Gene and Jodi Barbier designed and helped build their large contemporary wood home. It is partially hidden by tall pines in a peaceful country setting. Central to the house is a vast living area with a cathedral ceiling and vertical windows that span its full height. It is amazing how homey the huge space feels. There are decorative accents galore, a mighty wood-burning stove, and friendly hosts who take very good care of you. Attractively furnished guest rooms are on the upper level of the house. They open onto a walkway that overlooks the living area on three sides. The Barbiers invite you to "come and enjoy the peace, quiet, and beauty." You'll be glad you did.

Pets accommodated in basement; children welcome; full breakfast and treats; TV; kitchen and laundry privileges; crib; playpen; decks; bicycles; gym equipment; ski storage; Mount Shasta skiing (Nordic and downhill), Lake Shastina water sports, golf courses, and dinner houses in area; airport pickup (Weed, Dunsmuir, Montague). Room C is a loft with sofa bed.

Room	Bed	Bath	Entrance	Floor	Daily Rates S - D	(EP)
A	1D	Pvt	Main	2	$40-$45	($10)
B	1D	Pvt	Main	2	$40-$45	($10)
C	1Q	Pvt	Main	2	$40-$45	($10)

Gold
Country
&
the
Sierra

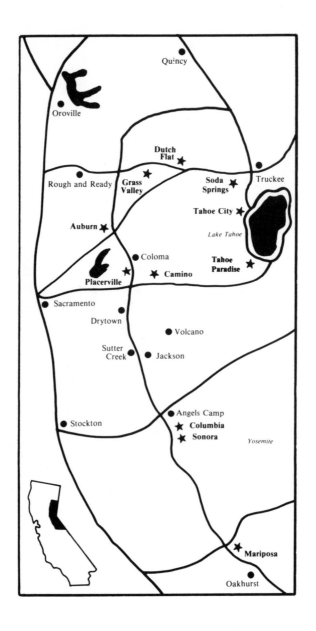

GOLD COUNTRY & the Sierra

Gold dust still seems to shimmer in the air of the Gold Country, as folded foothills and mahogany manzanita bask in the sun. Imagine: the whoops and hollers of a crowd gathered around the assayer's office as a nugget weighs in at one hundred ninety-five pounds. Imagine: banditos cresting one of these basking hills to descend on a passing stagecoach, their own version of the Gold Rush. Imagine: Mark Twain writing in a one-room cabin about a major sporting event he's just witnessed, a frog-jumping contest.

The northern gold mines centered around Nevada City and Grass Valley. Walking tours of these and nearby towns unearth some interesting stories about such characters as Lola Montez and Snowshoe Thompson and the secession of Rough and Ready from the Union in the 1850's. It joined up again in 1948, so you won't need a visa. In Grass Valley, the North Star Powerhouse Mine Museum has been called the best mining museum in the Gold Country.

At the eastern end of Nevada County, Truckee marks the gateway to Lake Tahoe. Writing postcards from here is a challenge. What more can be said of this pine-fringed blue eye of the high Sierra?

The seventy-one-mile drive around Lake Tahoe includes coves and casinos, mountains and marinas. Travelers can take their pick. Most people, however, would pick Emerald Bay. Scooped out by a massive glacier, it glitters brightly in its granite setting. At its southern tip is a replica of a Viking castle, authentic from its stone foundation to its sod roof. In winter, Lake Tahoe bundles up in snow and plays ski resort. Downhillers take to the steep slopes, while Nordic skiers make their way along the silent snow of the cross-country trails.

History buffs will strike it rich along the Gold Mine Trail, with towns like Sutter Creek, Jackson, Volcano, Amador City, and Drytown. (Dry as in Dry Creek; Drytown had twenty-six saloons in its heyday.) In Jackson, some travelers recommend a stop at St. Sava's Serbian Church and cemetery. The modest clapboard church is the mother church of the entire Western Hemisphere. What it lacks in size it makes up in dignity. An equally eloquent spirit resides at Indian Grinding Rock State Park, where descendants of California's original residents hold annual powwows in the fall.

Visitors to this area have a pleasant surprise in store for them if they have not heard of the rapidly growing wine industry here. The more than twenty wineries are often small, family-run establishments, making tastings a friendly and congenial experience.

The Gold Rush may be over, but Sonora, former hub of the southern mining district, has never taken a breather. Its hustling heritage blends well with its current role as county seat and trading center.

In Columbia, however, history marches in place. In this completely restored mining town, even people in sunglasses feel at home riding the stagecoach, drinking sarsaparilla, and eating Cornish pasties. Not too far away, Calaveras Big Trees State Park offers groves of giant sequoias and one of the loveliest rivers in California, the Stanislaus.

Daffodil Hill is a springtime (can we say it?) thrill. Over two hundred thousand of them trumpet spring. The competition from the wildflowers is stiff, though. Poppies, brodiaeas, lupines, larkspur, Mariposa lilies, mullein, and wild roses give their cultivated neighbors a run for their money.

To the southeast is California's gold mine of beauty, Yosemite National Park. Sheer walls of the glacier gorge rise almost vertically to four thousand feet above the peaceful meadows of the valley floor. In spring, plunging waterfalls veil chasms in perpetual mist. You walk tall in the high country, with its regal peaks and gem-like lakes, and feel small beneath the giant sequoias of the Mariposa Grove. One of the most spectacular spots for beauty in the country, Yosemite is a place for all seasons. The same could certainly be said of the Gold Country in general.

Dry Creek Bed & Breakfast   **(916) 878-0885**
13740 Dry Creek Road, Auburn, CA 95603
(Two miles west of I-80 and east of Highway 49)

Dry Creek B&B is nestled in the countryside just outside Auburn. The contemporary redwood home is situated on four wooded acres alongside a wild stream. The sounds of rushing water and birdsong are just about all you can hear in this setting of natural beauty. The accommodations include a luxurious three-room suite (bedroom, bath, and sitting room with a view of trees and stream) and a room with twin beds and a private bath. All guests have use of a large common room with a fireplace and of a lovely deck. Superb breakfasts are cooked to order and served at the convenience of guests. Although this home isn't far from major highways, other gold rush towns, and all sorts of outdoor recreation, it might as well be hours from civilization. The emphasis at Dry Creek is on privacy, comfort, and the world of nature. Why not get away to it all?

Dog (possibly) in residence; children by arrangement; full breakfast; AC; large library; refrigerator and laundry privileges; deck; scenic hikes and golf nearby; tennis, swimming, and racquetball free year-round at Racquet Club, five minutes away; some French spoken; airport pickup (Auburn). Brochure available. 10% discount for three days or longer.

Room	Bed	Bath	Entrance	Floor	Daily Rates S - D	(EP)
A	1Q	Pvt	Sep	1	$50-$55	
B	2T	Pvt	Main	1	$40-$45	

Lincoln House (916) 885-8880
191 Lincoln Way, Auburn, CA 95603
(Near I-80 and Foresthill Exit)

This charming little house has a storybook quality that sets a nostalgic tone. Its shingled exterior is painted blue with white trim. Crossing the bridge over the fishpond in front is a delightful prelude to the friendly welcome you'll get at Lincoln House. As you enter, there's a sitting room where afternoon refreshments are served by a stone fireplace. A sunny yellow guest room on the main floor looks out on the Koi-filled pond. Upstairs, you can choose between two rooms—the Shenandoah with a garden view and the Mary Todd with a small dormer room adjacent. Soft colors, handmade quilts, notable antiques, and personal touches create a cozy warmth throughout the house. A fine Continental breakfast is served in the dining room, where large windows frame a stunning view of Sierra majesty. If a swim sounds good, there's a pool and a cabana surrounded by gardens. In creating Lincoln House, Howard and Ginny Leal seem to have thought of everything their guests could want in a B&B.

Dog and two cats in residence; no pets; children over ten OK; smoking outside only; TV and VCR; AC; swimming pool; Spanish spoken; airport pickup (Auburn). Brochure available.

Room	Bed	Bath	Entrance	Floor	Daily Rates S - D	(EP)
A	1D	Pvt	Main	1	$35-$45	
B	2T or 1K	Pvt	Main	2	$45-$55	
C	1T & 1D	Pvt	Main	2	$45-$55	($10)

Old Auburn Bed & Breakfast   **(916) 885-6407**
149 Pleasant Avenue, Auburn, CA 95603
(Near Historic Old Auburn)

It's an easy stroll from this B&B to the central and oldest section of Auburn, which is all you'd expect a quaint gold rush town in the Sierra foothills to be. Many restored buildings are on view, and exploring the area on foot is a treat. Lodging at the Old Auburn helps you get into the spirit of the early days with old-fashioned touches—homemade desserts in the evening and rooms with the delectable names of Peach Cobbler, Fresh Cream, and Raspberry Tart. The rooms have ceiling fans and quaint furnishings, and the color schemes are appropriate to their names. Breakfast is served in the main floor dining room and afternoon wine in the comfortable parlor. Yes, staying at the Old Auburn is a sweet experience indeed.

No pets; children over twelve OK; smoking on veranda only; airport pickup (Auburn).

Room	Bed	Bath	Entrance	Floor	Daily Rates S - D	(EP)
A	1Q	Shd*	Main	2	$38-$45	
B	2T or 1K	Shd*	Main	2	$38-$45	
C	1T	Shd*	Main	2	$38	

Hollabrunn Homestead   **(916) 644-3832**
P.O. Box 196, Camino, CA 95709
(Just off Highway 50 between Sacramento and Lake Tahoe)

Picture a small log cabin tucked snugly into the wooded Sierra foothills, surrounded by eleven acres of trees and incredible serenity. Hollabrunn Homestead gives one a fascinating sense of history; it's hard to believe the twentieth century is going on outside. The original one-room structure with a loft and an added bathroom offers privacy for a person in need of solitude, romance for a couple, or fun for a small family. Kids can roam freely, get to know the resident farm animals, and fish in the trout pond. Hosts Lee and Maureen Chiusano, whose home is a few steps from the cabin, extend a hearty welcome to their neck of the woods.

No pets or smoking; families welcome; Apple Hill orchards, gold rush towns nearby; twin bed mattresses in loft for children. Brochure available.

Room	Bed	Bath	Entrance	Floor	Daily Rates S - D	(EP)
A	1D & 2T	Pvt	Sep	1 & 2	$45	($5)

Mt. Holly Estate   **(209) 532-0542**
P.O. Box 787, Columbia, CA 95310
(Just north of Columbia, off Parrotts Ferry Road)

Columbia has long been a favorite destination of anyone visiting the Mother Lode, especially private pilots. In the vicinity of the airport and Columbia State Park is Mt. Holly Estate, offering an opportunity to stay and get the full flavor of this quaint gold rush town. Hosts Paul and Jean Schweizer chose their location for its peaceful, secluded setting. Their home is truly one of a kind. The Tudor-influenced exterior gives no hint of what you'll find inside. The interior has a rustic, baronial elegance that is partially due to the Schweizers' taste for unusual, large antiques, fascinating memorabilia, and paintings of historical significance. Cathedral ceilings give the living room and den a vast, open feeling. Old wood has been used extensively for walls and doors; brass sconces lend a warm glow; stone, brick, and tile create a rich, textured appearance. From the living room picture window, the scenic countryside is in full view. Sunsets from this vantage point are an inspiration. Lodging at Mt. Holly Estate will make your visit to Columbia unforgettable.

No pets or children; smoking outside only; TV; AC; swimming pool; picnics prepared at an extra charge; airport pickup (Columbia). *Reservations required two weeks in advance.*

Room	Bed	Bath	Entrance	Floor	Daily Rates S - D	(EP)
A	1Q	Shd*	Main	1	$55	

Elmore Hill Mine   **(916) 389-2363**
P.O. Box 190, Dutch Flat, CA 95714
(Two miles from I-80 between Alta and Dutch Flat)

The town of Dutch Flat was the center of extensive mining in the 1850's and later was a strategic way point in the building of the transcontinental railroad. Nestled deep in the woods not far from Dutch Flat is the home of Sally and Nicolaas Pansegrouw. It is set on a ridge of forested land between the Bear and Little Bear Rivers and was built in 1902 by Sally's grandfather as headquarters for a hydraulic mine operation. The interior of the house has a rich, permanent quality unmatched in newer homes. The Pansegrouws have finished off the upper floor of the pitched-roof house, creating a gallery lined with hundreds of books, a large bedroom, and a bath. There's another guest room with private bath downstairs. Historical explorations, river recreation, hiking, and Nordic skiing can be enjoyed while staying at Elmore Hill Mine. It's a wonderful getaway even if you do nothing more than sit and take it easy on the vine-covered front porch.

Dog, cat, and parrot in residence; no pets; families welcome.

Room	Bed	Bath	Entrance	Floor	Daily Rates S - D	(EP)
A	3T	Pvt	Main	2	$40-$45	($10)
B	1D	Pvt	Main	1	$30-$35	

Annie Horan's Bed & Breakfast   **(916) 272-2418**
415 West Main Street, Grass Valley, CA 95945
(Two blocks from center of town)

The charming Queen Anne home of Ivan and Bette Nance looks like an ad for Grass Valley's unique Victorian Christmas. It's a two-story confection, complete with gingerbread trim, displaying superior design and workmanship. The Nances have collected antiques from far and near that best depict the elegant era of the gold country's heyday. Previous owner Annie Horan offered fine lodging here for over fifty years. She would no doubt approve of the gracious treatment guests receive today. Breakfast is served each morning in the dining room or in the fresh mountain air on the spacious deck. Many historical points are within walking distance, and a shuttle bus takes visitors on various routes around the area. People come to Grass Valley for a number of reasons—to soak up some history, to visit the Empire Mine, to experience a Victorian Christmas, to attend a Bluegrass Festival. Whatever *your* reason, the Nances would be pleased to have you as their guest.

Dog in residence; no pets, children, or smoking; airport pickup (Nevada County). Brochure available. Rates are $50 (A,B,D) and $40 (C) midweek, except holidays.

Room	Bed	Bath	Entrance	Floor	Daily Rates S - D	(EP)
A	1Q	Pvt	Main	2	$75	
B	1Q	Pvt	Main	2	$70	
C	1D	Pvt	Main	2	$50	
D	1Q	Pvt	Main	2	$70	

Domike's Bed & Breakfast   **(916) 273-9010**
220 Colfax Avenue, Grass Valley, CA 95945
(In town, just off Highway 49 on Route 174)

Don and Joyce Domike undertook quite a job when they set out to restore one of Grass Valley's largest and most impressive Victorians. The town is glad they did. The house is set back from the street in an elevated position in keeping with its status. Huge old trees and a lovely lawn are enclosed by a traditional white picket fence. Inside, the Domikes keep the atmosphere pretty casual and are prone to conversation of travel and good books. The upstairs accommodations are appointed with down comforters, clawfoot tubs, and Casablanca fans. Rooms C and D have beds with canopies. You certainly can't go hungry at Domike's. They offer late afternoon beverages and nibbles, plus a hearty breakfast in the morning. Hosts try in every way to make sure your stay in Grass Valley is a satisfying one.

No pets; families welcome; full breakfast; hot or cold lunches packed to go; rollaway bed and crib available; public transportation; airport pickup (Grass Valley). Rooms A and B can be rented together at a lower rate.

Room	Bed	Bath	Entrance	Floor	Daily Rates S - D	(EP)
A	2T	Shd*	Main	2	$45	($10)
B	1K	Shd*	Main	2	$55	($10)
C	1Q	Pvt	Main	2	$60	($10)
D	1K	Pvt	Main	2	$65	($10)

Doris & Michael Beccio   **(209) 742-6206**
4160 Vista Grande Way, Mariposa, CA 95338
(Just off Highway 140, four miles southwest of Mariposa)

    The approach to the Beccios' home along sun-dappled Yaqui Gulch
Road takes you through rolling cattle country dotted with live oaks. It's a
world of remote beauty—a wonderful discovery. The Beccios offer guests the
entire ground floor of their rustic cedar home. This includes a huge den with a
wood-burning stove, a dining area, two bedrooms, and a bath. But as far as
I'm concerned, the pièce de résistance is a small room with handcrafted redwood walls that contains a large hydro-spa tub. Superb views are yours from
the den, bedrooms, and deck. As a vacation headquarters or a short stopover,
the Beccios' home has a lot to recommend it.

    Dog in residence; children over ten welcome; generous, deluxe breakfast
served on deck seasonally; refreshments served on arrival; AC. ****KNIGHT-
TIME PUBLICATIONS SPECIAL RATE:** 10% discount with this book.

Room	Bed	Bath	Entrance	Floor	Daily Rates S - D	(EP)
A	2T & 1D	Pvt	Sep	1G	$30-$45	($12)

Dick & Shirl's Bed & Breakfast　　　　　　　　　　　**(209) 966-2514**
4870 Triangle Road, Mariposa, CA 95338
(Five miles from Mariposa enroute to Yosemite)

Hosts Dick and Shirl Fiester are quite contented living on their fifteen forested acres. It's a quiet, secluded setting where you can slow down, unwind, and tune in to nature—most people leave completely refreshed. The home itself is rustic, commodious, and very relaxing. On the main floor, there's an open living area with a large, stone fireplace and cathedral ceilings of warm, polished redwood. An open kitchen is adjacent, and just off the kitchen is a guest suite that can be closed off for complete privacy. Large breakfasts and friendly conversation are part of the gracious hospitality to be found here. For country lodging on the way to Yosemite (forty miles away), Dick and Shirl's is a fine choice.

Dog and cat in residence; no pets; TV; barbecue.

Room	Bed	Bath	Entrance	Floor	Daily Rates S - D	(EP)
A	2T	Pvt	Main	1G	$40	

Granny's Garden   **(209) 377-8342**
7333 Highway 49 N, Bear Valley, Mariposa, CA 95338
(Twelve miles northwest of Mariposa)

For as long as anyone in Bear Valley remembers, this small Victorian farmhouse has been known as "Granny's." Built in 1896, it was the home of Dave Trabucco's grandparents. After years of restoration, Dave and his wife Dixie use the house for B&B lodging. (Their own home is on the property.) There are two guest rooms on the main floor; they share a split bathroom, complete with clawfoot tub. A totally private upstairs suite includes a bedroom, bath, sitting room, and balcony. Many antiques in the house are original furnishings. A stitchery on the wall of Granny's room (B) reads: "May This House To Every Guest Be A Place Of Cheer And Rest." Dixie continues the hospitable tradition with elegant, special touches like flowers, wine, and nice serving pieces set on a lace tablecloth. The area surrounding Bear Valley is rich in history and gold rush lore, and the fishing is good at nearby Bagby. But if I were a guest, I think I'd spend a fair amount of time relaxing in a rocker on Granny's front porch.

Dogs, cats, and farm animals on property; no pets or children; two porches (one front and one screened); nearby Bon Ton Cafe serves Guatemalan and American food; airport pickup (Mariposa). *Open Mother's Day-Halloween.*

Room	Bed	Bath	Entrance	Floor	Daily Rates S - D	(EP)
A	2T	Shd*	Sep	1	$35-$40	
B	1D	Shd*	Main	1	$40	
C	1D	Pvt	Sep	2	$50	

The Homestead

(209) 966-2820

P.O. Box 13, Midpines, CA 95345
(Eight miles from Mariposa enroute to Yosemite)

The Homestead isn't the place for a quick stopover. You need some time just to take in the good fortune of having found it, and I promise that you won't want to leave when the time comes. This is a B&B with unusual character and privacy. It's a restored rustic ranch where you'll have an entire house to yourself. Downstairs there's a living room with a big stone fireplace, a well stocked kitchen, and a large master bedroom and bath. Two smaller bedrooms and a half-bath are upstairs. Enjoy all this *plus* the superlative hospitality of hosts Blair and Helen Fowler, whose home is across a wide meadow from The Homestead. One could easily spend several blissful days in the woodland setting and utter peacefulness of this getaway abode.

Barnyard has ducks; horses graze nearby; barbecue; trails; some German and French spoken; airport pickup (Mariposa). Ask about family and weekly rates. Two-night minimum on weekends.

Room	Bed	Bath	Entrance	Floor	Daily Rates S - D	(EP)
A	1Q	Pvt	Sep	1	$50	($20)
	3T	½ Shd*		2		

Meadow Creek Ranch   **(209) 966-3843**
2669 Triangle Road, Mariposa, CA 95338
(Twelve miles south of Mariposa at Highway 49 S and Triangle Road)

"A pleasant haven of rest" reads the description of this 1858 home in a book on the history of Mariposa. It was once a stop on the Mariposa-Oakhurst stagecoach run that provided overnight lodging for weary travelers. Though many improvements have been made for the sake of comfort, guests today feel the same welcoming spirit of the early days. Hosts Bob and Carol Shockley want you to feel completely at home here, whether you're relaxing in the cozy living room or strolling around the lovely grounds. Guests have a choice of four charming bedrooms, each decorated with a mixture of country and European flavors. After a hard day of traveling, or of exploring the wonder that is Yosemite, you'll be glad to return to this "pleasant haven of rest."

No pets or children; full breakfast; seasonal refreshments served on arrival; Visa and Master Card accepted. Also available is a "Country Cottage" with private bath, kitchenette, and queen bed with canopy at $85.

Room	Bed	Bath	Entrance	Floor	Daily Rates S - D	(EP)
A	1Q	Shd*	Main	2	$55	
B	1Q	Shd*	Main	2	$55	
C	2T	Shd*	Main	2	$55	
D	1D	Shd*	Main	1	$55	

The Pelennor   **(209) 966-2832**
3871 Highway 49 S, Mariposa, CA 95338   **or 966-5353**
(Five miles south of Mariposa at Bootjack)

     Dick and Gwen Foster follow the Scottish tradition of offering simple, low-cost accommodations, which are now in a new building adjacent to their home. They can provide tips on enjoying the area, a bit of hospitality, and even some bagpipe tunes on request. Hosts are instructors of the St. Andrews Pipe Band, and Dick is an avid stargazer. No other B&B that I know of specializes in "Stars and Pipes," but guests who have sampled this unique combination are not likely to forget it. Each morning the Fosters serve what they term "a solid breakfast." For informal lodgings just off the main route of the Mother Lode, The Pelennor makes a welcome stop for the passing traveler.

     Hosts have dog and cat; other animals roam through property; smoking outside only. At most, two rooms share one bath. Two extra bedrooms in main house available as needed. Brochure available.

Room	Bed	Bath	Entrance	Floor	Daily Rates S - D	(EP)
A	1Q	Shd*	Sep	2	$20-$25	($5)
B	1Q	Shd*	Sep	2	$20-$25	($5)
C	1D	Shd*	Sep	2	$20-$25	($5)
D	2T	Shd*	Sep	2	$20-$25	($5)

Tanglewood   **(209) 742-7851**
3165 Wass Road, Mariposa, CA 95338
(Ten miles south of Mariposa, off Highway 49 S)

Tanglewood is the home of Jim and Muriel Powers, whose guests are made to feel welcome in the truest sense of the word. Despite the home's conventional outward appearance, the interior is alive with the aura of times past. Antiques and collectibles have been chosen with keen sensibility. They are enhanced by Jim's handcrafted woodwork throughout the house. Guests are offered a large Victorian bed/sitting room or a smaller room with twin beds. Anyone with a penchant for music of the Big Band era will be impressed with the hosts' extensive record collection. Muriel gives tours of the Mariposa Courthouse and can share her considerable knowledge of local history with interested guests. I've been saving the best till last: Tanglewood is remarkably situated so that you can relax on the deck and look out across a panorama of mountains toward the deepening hues of the sunset. Such perfection is hard to come by.

No pets; choice of shower or tub bath; breakfast suited to tastes and schedule of guests; limited French, Slavic, and German spoken; airport pickup (Mariposa).

Room	Bed	Bath	Entrance	Floor	Daily Rates S - D	(EP)
A	1D	Pvt	Main	1	$30-$35	($10)
B	2T	Pvt	Main	1	$30-$35	($10)

Chichester House   **(916) 626-1882**
2908 Wood Street, Placerville, CA 95667
(Historic district, two blocks from downtown)

Placerville has its share of impressive historic homes, but Chichester House is surely one of the most handsome. Perched on a hill with lovely old trees around it, the late Victorian house is comfortably elegant rather than stiff and formal. The porches, parlor, and library are inviting places to enjoy a good book or a conversation. The home's fine woodwork and three fireplaces give a glowing warmth to the interior. Guest rooms are individually decorated with antiques, some of which are family heirlooms. A delightful personality has been created for each room through the use of color and nostalgia pieces. Nan Carson takes great care in serving a special breakfast in the dining room each morning. She'll succeed in making your stay as memorable as Chichester House itself.

No pets, smoking, or RV parking; children by arrangement; full breakfast; AC; main bath shared (robes provided); half-bath in each room; airport pickup (Placerville). 10% discount Sunday-Thursday nights. Brochure available.

Room	Bed	Bath	Entrance	Floor	Daily Rates S - D	(EP)
A	1T & 1D	½ Pvt	Main	2	$50-$60	($10)
B	1D	½ Pvt	Main	2	$45-$55	
C	1D	½ Pvt	Main	2	$45-$55	

River Rock Home   **(916) 622-7640**
1756 Georgetown Road, Placerville, CA 95667
(Three miles from Placerville via Route 193)

Located directly on the South Fork of the American River, the home of Dorothy Irvin is very quiet and peaceful. From three of the lovely, antique-furnished guest rooms, you can be at eye level with the river flowing by as you lie in bed. An expansive deck stretches by each room, with patio doors opening onto it. Deluxe breakfasts are served here in summer, and there are plenty of lounge chairs for sunbathing. River rafting, fishing, and panning for gold are popular warm-weather activities. In winter there's still lots to do, such as exploring gold rush towns, wine-tasting in foothill wineries, and skiing in Sierra resorts. It's nice, too, having a fireside breakfast in the living room. Dorothy goes out of her way to make sure that her guests are pleased and comfortable.

Two dogs in residence; no pets; children by arrangement; full breakfast; AC; TV; laundry privileges; hot tub; rafting trips arranged; extra meals possible; airport pickup (Placerville). Rooms A, B, and D face the river; C has a vanity-sink; D is a suite that could sleep four at $75.

Room	Bed	Bath	Entrance	Floor	Daily Rates S - D	(EP)
A	1D	Shd*	Main	1	$55	
B	1D	Shd*	Main	1	$55	
C	1D	Shd*	Main	1	$55	
D	1Q	Pvt	Main	1	$65	

A Room at the Top **(916) 426-3211**
P.O. Box 305, Soda Springs, CA 95728
(Castle Peak Exit from I-80, Donner Summit area)

Suzanne Henderson handles the townhouse rentals at Boreal Village and has two B&B rooms on the lower level of her own home in the complex. They are well separated from the main living quarters, so guests can come and go with ease through the entrance near their rooms. Suzanne always makes you feel welcome to sit by the woodstove upstairs and enjoy the view of lake and mountains while you make your plans or take it easy after an active day. Many people come to Boreal for the skiing. Slopes abound in the area, and you can cross-country ski right from the door! Summer can be just as busy. There are hiking trails galore, tennis, rafting, mountain climbing, historical explorations, as well as fishing, water-skiing, and swimming at Donner Lake. A Room at the Top offers lodging in a congenial atmosphere amidst the stunning peaks of Donner Summit.

Dog in residence; small pets OK; full breakfast; TV; kitchen privileges by arrangement; sofa bed in Room A (no extra charge for use); airport pickup (Truckee and Reno in summer only; extra charge). Brochure available. During winter, weekend and holiday rates are $10 higher. May not be available during May and September.

Room	Bed	Bath	Entrance	Floor	Daily Rates S - D (EP)
A	1Q	Shd*	Main	1G	$25-$40
B	1Q	Shd*	Main	1G	$25-$40

Jameson's   **(209) 532-1248**
22157 Feather River Drive, Sonora, CA 95370
(Off Highway 108, Crystal Falls area)

Virg and Jean Birdsall combed California for the perfect spot to start their bed and breakfast venture, and the search certainly paid off. The house rests among trees and boulders in the scenic Crystal Falls area east of Sonora. The Birdsalls have stayed in B&Bs and pensiones in Europe, the U.S., South America, and Mexico. Their decor and hospitality reflect the best aspects of their travel experiences. Each guest room is named for a woman immortalized in song—"Charmaine" (French), "Kathleen" (Irish), "Maria Elena" (Mexican), and "Scheherazade" (a bridal suite with an exotic Arabian Nights theme). Breakfast may be served on the large deck amidst trees, birds, and the sound of a nearby waterfall. There's a game room with pool table and a living room with cathedral ceilings and fireplace to enjoy when you're not out and about. Jameson's is a place where you can just take it easy and let yourself be pampered.

No pets or children; smoking on decks only; robes provided; Room A has waterfall view; B, C, and D open to deck; A, B, and C are $5 more on weekends; town of Twain Harte nearby; good access to Dodge Ridge and Pinecrest via Highway 108; some Spanish spoken; airport pickup (Columbia). Brochure available.

Room	Bed	Bath	Entrance	Floor	Daily Rates S - D	(EP)
A	1D	Shd*	Sep	1	$40	
B	2T or 1K	Shd*	Sep	1	$45	
C	1Q	Shd*	Sep	1	$45	
D	1Q	Shd*	Sep	1	$60	

Via Serena Ranch   **(209) 532-5307**
18007 Via Serena, Sonora, CA 95370
(Between Sonora and Jamestown)

Set on beautiful rolling acreage that only *seems* miles from anywhere, Via Serena Ranch is ideally located for sampling the old-west flavor of the historic mining towns of Jamestown and Columbia. Sonora, a hub of activity, is just moments away. While you're exploring this rich and varied area, Beverly Ballash will make you feel truly welcome in her elegant ranch-style home. Here you'll find comfortable, immaculate accommodations and a breakfast to remember. Each guest room is a work of art. It's difficult choosing among them, but I found the one with an English hunting theme particularly striking. A large living room and a deck are yours for reading, socializing, or just relaxing. In every way possible, the climate is always perfect at Via Serena Ranch.

No pets, children, or smoking; TV; AC; robes provided; airport pickup (Columbia). Brochure available.

Room	Bed	Bath	Entrance	Floor	Daily Rates S - D	(EP)
A	2T	Shd*	Main	1G	$43	
B	1Q	Shd*	Main	1G	$45	
C	1Q	Shd*	Main	1G	$48	

Cedar Tree   **(916) 583-5421**
P.O. Box 7106, Tahoe City, CA 95730
(Between Highway 89 and Lake Tahoe)

    Walt and Doris Genest make it easy for their guests to enjoy Lake Tahoe in a variety of ways. Cedar Tree, an aptly named mountain retreat, is just a short distance from a private beach and pier on the lake. You can try your luck at fishing with Walt in his boat, or at other games of chance in the North Shore casinos. Golfing, boating, cycling on trails, hiking, rafting, skiing, and fine dining are all possible in the vicinity of Cedar Tree. The Genests' daughter Margret sometimes babysits with children of guests. The second floor loft, with cable TV and extra beds, is popular with the younger set. Doris takes pride in serving nourishing homemade treats for breakfast. If you're looking for a vacation spot with the comforts of home *and* lots of things to do close by, Cedar Tree hits the jackpot.

    Bird in residence; children, kitchen privileges, and fishing by special advance arrangement; barbecue; deck; hot tub. Rooms A and B have sinks. Two-night minimum on weekends. *Cedar Tree is open for B&B April-November.*

Room	Bed	Bath	Entrance	Floor	Daily Rates S - D	(EP)
A	1Q	Shd*	Main	2	$40	
B	2T	Shd*	Main	2	$40	
C	1Q	Pvt	Main	1	$40	

Lakeside House   **(916) 583-8796**
P.O. Box 7108, Tahoe City, CA 95730
(1745 Sequoia, beside Lake Tahoe)

Jim and Suni Kreft have taken exquisite care in creating the special atmosphere they wanted at Lakeside House. The 1916 gambrel home now offers some of Lake Tahoe's finest lodging, combining historic elegance and a boating theme. Each of four upstairs bedrooms is named for a steam-powered craft from the lake's past. I found the color schemes particularly appealing. My large bed with fluffy comforter was hard to get out of in the morning, but the promise of the sumptuous breakfast awaiting me provided just the needed catalyst. You can view the lake from your bed in the Nevada Room or from the Lakeview Room, a relaxing place for guests that occupies the front of the second floor. People also enjoy gathering in the downstairs living room, with its boxed-beam ceiling, huge stone fireplace, and warm polished wood. Even with Tahoe's amazing variety of activities to choose from in every season, I warn you, it's not easy to leave Lakeside House.

Dog in residence; no pets; no children, except in cabin; smoking on patio deck; full breakfast; afternoon refreshments; sitting room; library; board games; private beach for guests. A private cabin, completely self-contained, is available for families; inquire about rates. Brochure available.

Room	Bed	Bath	Entrance	Floor	Daily Rates S - D	(EP)
A	1Q	Shd*	Main	2	$65	
B	1Q	Shd*	Main	2	$65	
C	1Q	Shd*	Main	2	$70	
D	1Q	½ Pvt	Main	2	$75	

Chalet A-Capella   **(916) 577-6841**
P.O. Box 11334, Tahoe Paradise, CA 95708
(Near intersection of Highways 89 and 50)

    Richard and Suzanne Capella's chalet-style home blends well with the Alpine scenery that surrounds it. You can go cross-country skiing from the doorstep, drive to a number of ski touring trails or downhill slopes in about thirty minutes, or fish right across the street in the Upper Truckee River. South Shore casinos are a short distance away. The interior woodwork and sloped ceilings of the upstairs guest quarters create a snug, rustic feeling. Two bedrooms and a shared bath are just right for a family or two couples. Summer or winter, Chalet A-Capella is a picture-perfect vacation spot.

    No pets; children by arrangement; no smoking preferred; TV; deck; twin beds are extra long; Italian spoken; two-night minimum preferred; $5 extra charge for one-night stays.

Room	Bed	Bath	Entrance	Floor	Daily Rates S - D	(EP)
A	2T	Shd*	Sep	2	$40	
B	1Q	Shd*	Sep	2	$45	

Wise, cultivated, genial con-

versation is the last flower of

civilization. . . . Conversation is

our account of ourselves.

—Ralph Waldo Emerson

What is pleasanter than the tie

of host and guest?

—Aeschylus

Southern
California

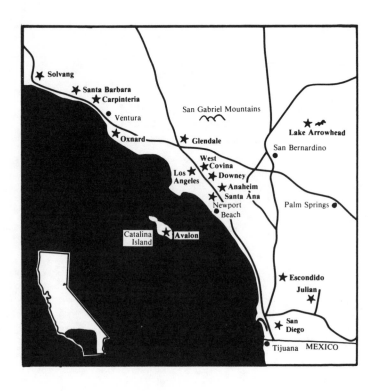

California is a little like Shangri-La, a paradise that is sometimes hard to find. But visitors to Santa Barbara will feel that they have found it. Palm trees, sunny beaches, technicolor sails on blue water, red rooftops and white stucco against a gray-green backdrop of mountains—it's all here, the California of the travel posters. No wonder this was the place chosen as Shangri-La for the original movie version of *Lost Horizons*.

Santa Barbara is a city at home with itself, as a ramble along the terrazzo walks will convince you. A side trip through the County Courthouse buildings will make you feel as if you are in a Moorish castle. Turrets, arched doorways, and curving staircases have a regal air, a mood matched by the exquisitely manicured gardens. From the clocktower, a panorama of city and sea lies below. Another must-see is the "Queen of Missions," one of California's most beautiful, situated alongside a reflecting pool where mission Indians once bathed. Santa Barbara's peaceful pace makes it a good place to relax or gather your energies before heading south to L.A.

L.A. may be the only city in the country known by its initials. Somehow that fits. It expresses the adolescent charm of the unpredictable and offbeat that you find here. It makes this sprawling city of four hundred sixty square miles and three million people seem both down-home casual and fast-lane exciting.

Many people are not sure just where L.A. is—exactly. Is it downtown near the Civic Center and the Music Center's cultural constellation of theaters and auditoriums? Or is it more toward the soundstages of the satellite TV and movie studios? Maybe it's over near Chinatown, Little Tokyo, or Olvera Street, that delightful, brick-paved pedestrian street with its colorful wares of serapes and ollas, its taste-tempters of biznaga (candied cactus) or green corn tamales. Wait, isn't it somewhere over on Hollywood Boulevard near Mann's Chinese Theater, where the stars leave footprints? It can't be far from Griffith Park, three thousand acres supporting a zoo, a planetarium, an outdoor theater, stables, playgrounds, and a mountain wilderness. Or is L.A., as some wags suggest, the La Brea Tar Pits where life-sized models of prehistoric animals (the real skeletons are in the Museum of Natural History) rise from the black murk, as Mercedes Benzes and Porsches whiz by on Wilshire Boulevard? But what about the beaches? Don't all of L.A.'s streets lead to the beach?

After you visit L.A., you will undoubtedly have your own opinion about its location. No one leaves L.A. without an opinion.

Northeast of L.A. the San Gabriel Mountains stand sentinel to Glendale and other small cities, looking austere from the suburban streets. But a drive through these mountains reveals a wealth of waterfalls, rocky ravines, old gold mines, and Indian trails. Further east is Riverside, birthplace of the multi-million-dollar navel orange industry. You can see one of the two original trees brought from Brazil in 1873. It is still bearing fruit on the corner of Magnolia and Arlington Streets.

South of L.A., from Huntington Beach to San Clemente, is the Gold

Coast of California. Whether this coastline is named for the golden tans acquired here or the high price of real estate is in dispute. Either way, the Gold Coast offers a variety of beach topography. Wide, sandy stretches, cliff-clutched coves, tidepools, and balmy breezes delight the senses; swimming, boating, fishing, surfing, scuba diving; snorkeling, and windsurfing strain them to the limit. For your more artistic sensibilities, be sure to stop at the famous artists' colony in Laguna Beach.

For all its glory, the Gold Coast is actually the lesser-known side of Orange County, thanks to the magic wand of Walt Disney. In addition to Disneyland, which needs no description, there are three major amusement parks and seven specialty museums. The area roughly flanking Highway 5 is a never-ending world's fair. From Knott's Berry Farm (it was an actual farm once) north of Santa Ana down to Lion Country Safari, visitors will be amused, entertained, and informed. Aircraft, crocodiles, roller coasters, Wild West shows, chimps, antique cars—it's up to you to cry "Uncle."

Continuing oceanside to the south, you come—of course—to Oceanside. Watch the blue Pacific's lacy hem rise and fall, a slave not to fashion but to time. Oceanside is a good base for an exploration of San Diego's back country, a peaceful landscape including rambling hills, rocky peaks, and desert. Mission San Luis Rey, crowned "King of the Missions" as California's largest, dominates a hill overlooking a tranquil valley.

La Jolla, Jewel of the Pacific, has seven miles of coves, caves, and cliffs that are unsurpassed in the southland. On its northern boundary lies Torrey Pines State Park, where this Ice Age tree can be seen in abundance. Modern Icaruses in brightly colored wings hang-glide off the cliffs here.

La Jolla is the quiet edge of San Diego. In San Diego, the park came first; the city built up around it. Century-old Balboa Park is one of the country's greatest. Nine museums, the Old Globe Theater, and the renowned San Diego Zoo all lie within a public garden of fragrant eucalyptus trees and lush greenery. San Diego's other park, the Mission Bay Aquatic Park, is a water playground near downtown. Water sports and Sea World, a park within a park, are big attractions here. A stroll through Old Town is a stroll through San Diego's past. Nearby San Diego Mission was California's first.

With the diversity of natural and manmade attractions in Southern California, few generalizations apply. Only one seems certain: You will never run out of things to do.

Anaheim Bed & Breakfast   **(714) 533-1884**
1327 South Hickory, Anaheim, CA 92805
(Off Santa Ana Freeway, Ball Road Exit)

Anaheim is the obvious headquarters for anyone planning to visit Disneyland, which is less than a mile away, or Knott's Berry Farm. A guest at Anaheim Bed & Breakfast told me it was also easy to get to the beaches and L.A., as well as points south and east. (Clearly, he'd found the location ideal!) Margot Wright's suburban home exudes a friendly, welcoming quality that puts visitors at ease right away. She speaks German fluently and loves meeting people from all over the world. You'll be in good hands with this long-time resident of Anaheim—she knows the area intimately and can give you a real insider's view of things.

No pets or smoking; TV, AC, and fireplace in den and Room A; full breakfast on weekends; German spoken; good public transportation and airport connections.

Room	Bed	Bath	Entrance	Floor	Daily Rates S - D	(EP)
A	1D	Shd*	Main	1G	$25-$35	
B	2T	Shd*	Main	1G	$25-$35	

George & Jean Harris   **(805) 684-5629**
1483 Anita Street, Carpinteria, CA 93013
(One-half mile north of U.S. 101, Linden Exit)

    The Harrises couldn't be happier living in Carpinteria. "Our climate is heavenly!" says Jean. Their home is in a small suburban area surrounded by rolling ranchlands where flowers, fruit, and nursery stock grow in profusion. There are mountains in the background, and "The World's Safest Beach" is only a mile away. Nearby Abbey Gardens has the largest display of cacti in the country. Guests are offered a bedroom and a private bath in this comfortable, well-kept home. They're invited to use the croquet game on the back lawn and a spa that is set amidst ferns and flowers. Getting to know people as nice as the Harrises adds a lot to any vacation.

    No pets or RV parking; older child OK; smoking outside only; full breakfast; TV; spa.

Room	Bed	Bath	Entrance	Floor	Daily Rates S - D	(EP)
A	1K	Pvt	Main	1G	$30-$35	

D&B Schroeder Ranch   **(805) 684-1579**
1825 Cravens Lane, Carpinteria, CA 93013
(One mile from U.S. 101)

    The Schroeder Ranch, which produces avocados and other fruits, has an ocean view from the foothills of Carpinteria. There is a private accommodation for guests in the contemporary wood home, and it's equipped to make your stay cozy and complete. Some people like to explore the ten-acre ranch, finding fruit trees and a year-round creek. Others prefer to stay put and enjoy the sun and the view from the deck. For travelers wishing to thoroughly unwind, there is a spa in a lush, tropical setting. Hosts Bev and Don Schroeder sometimes engage in lively conversation, a bridge game, or tennis with their guests. In this hospitable atmosphere, your visit is sure to be a sterling experience.

    No smoking; TV; small refrigerator. The Schroeders also have a beach condo (across from "The World's Safest Beach") which is available by the day or week as a vacation rental. Inquiries welcome.

Room	Bed	Bath	Entrance	Floor	Daily Rates S - D	(EP)
A	1Q	Pvt	Sep	1	$50	($10)

Gull House   **(213) 510-2547**
P.O. Box 1381, Avalon, CA 90704   **or 257-1281**
(A short walk from bay and town)

       Whether you're discovering the romance of Santa Catalina for the first time or returning for the fiftieth, you'll find bed and breakfast at Gull House an experience unique on the island. Hosts Hattie and Bob Michalis offer two deluxe suites on the lower level of their contemporary home. Each unit has a separate entrance, a large living room with a gas log fireplace, a morning room with a refrigerator and table, a bedroom, and a bath. Accommodations are immaculate and nicely decorated. Have breakfast at your leisure under an Italian umbrella on the patio where there's a pool, spa, and a gas barbecue. It's an easy walk to reach many of the sights and activities for which the island is known. The distinct Mediterranean flavor of Catalina makes it a feast for the senses. And the hospitality at Gull House will add an extra dimension of comfort to your visit.

       No pets or children; TV and stereo in each suite; swimming pool; spa; tours, golfing, and horseback riding nearby; taxi service from ferry terminal. *Rates vary according to season and minimum stays. Per diem double occupancy charges range from $65 to $105; average is around $85; call or write for rate schedule with prepayment and cancellation conditions. **KNIGHT-TIME PUBLICATIONS SPECIAL RATE: 10% discount with this book.

Room	Bed	Bath	Entrance	Floor	Daily Rates S - D (EP)
A	1Q	Pvt	Sep	LL	*/**
B	1Q	Pvt	Sep	LL	See notes

The Lamplighters   **(213) 928-8229**
7724 East Cecilia Street, Downey, CA 90241
(One and one-half miles southwest of I-5 at Paramount)

If you're going to L.A. to see the major sights—from Universal Studios to Disneyland to the Queen Mary and Spruce Goose—you'd do well to pick this centrally located B&B in Downey. It's in a quiet suburb just south of L.A. with good access to the freeways you'll need. The Lamplighters is the home of Jim and Doris Gentry, avid B&B-ers themselves, who extend a warm welcome and the kinds of amenities that really make a difference when you're on the road. A cheerful front bedroom and private bath are the main guest quarters (A). Hospitable touches abound: flowers, fruit, and sherry in the room; terry robes in the closet for after swimming; afternoon wine and hors d'oeuvres; an expanded Continental breakfast attractively served in the dining room. The large pool and landscaped patio invite a refreshing pause after a busy day in the L.A. area. In every way, The Lamplighters is a nice place to come home to.

Two dogs in residence; no pets; teens (over sixteen) welcome; remote control TV in each room; extra bed available for fourth person in party; swimming pool (heated in warmer months) and patio.

Room	Bed	Bath	Entrance	Floor	Daily Rates S - D	(EP)
A	1D	Pvt	Main	1	$35-$40	
B	1T	Shd	Main	1	$30	($10)

Crickett's Bed & Breakfast   **(619) 741-5177**
1621 Gary Lane, Escondido, CA 92026
(Just north of Escondido, El Norte Exit from I-15)

    Enjoy the relaxing beauty of a country club setting when you stay at Crickett's Bed & Breakfast. Located just off the club's golf course, Crickett's offers golfers and tennis players a real vacation treat. Two upstairs bedrooms, each with private bath and remote control TV, make very pleasant accommodations for guests. Step out the back door to a patio with a large pool and spa, where you can take it easy in the sun. Your host, Marty Ricketts, collects Mexican and Oriental art objects. The vast white walls and open spaces in her contemporary home create a perfect backdrop for displaying the collection. Even though the beach and San Diego are only thirty minutes away, the environment and hospitality at Crickett's are likely to keep you from venturing too far afield.

    Dog in residence; no pets or children; TV and phone in each room; swimming pool with spa; tennis, golf, and dining at nearby country club; airport pickup (Palomar, or Lindbergh at a nominal charge). Master bedroom on main floor available as required.

Room	Bed	Bath	Entrance	Floor	Daily Rates S - D	(EP)
A	2T	Pvt	Main	2	$40-$45	
B	1D	Pvt	Main	2	$40-$45	

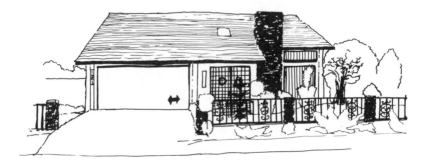

Halbig's Hacienda (619) 745-1296
432 South Citrus Avenue, Escondido, CA 92027
(East of town, off Valley Parkway)

The Halbigs came to Escondido in the fifties and the town literally grew up around them. The home that they built by hand sits on a knoll, removed from the hustle bustle, with wonderful views of the surrounding mountains. Fruit trees dot the property. Long verandas, adobe brick construction, and hand-hewn wooden doors recall the days of the early California ranchos. Three rooms are available for bed and breakfast; Room B has an heirloom brass bed. Ancestors of the Halbigs were dollmakers in Bavaria, and a few cherished antique dolls are on display. Escondido makes a good base for exploring San Diego's back country, fishing in nearby lakes, dropping by the Wild Animal Park, or paying a visit to Lawrence Welk's village and dinner theater. Beaches are only twenty minutes away, and San Diego forty-five. Enjoy a quiet, country-like atmosphere on the edge of town when you visit Halbig's Hacienda.

Children and pets welcome; TV; some Spanish spoken; airport pickup (Palomar). Inquire about discounts for extended stays.

Room	Bed	Bath	Entrance	Floor	Daily Rates S - D	(EP)
A	1Q	Shd*	Main	1G	$35	
B	1D	Shd*	Main	1G	$30	
C	2T	Shd*	Main	1G	$15-$30	

Geraldine & Spencer Shroff (818) 507-0774
1114 Park Avenue, Glendale, CA 91205
(South of Ventura Freeway and east of Golden State)

The Shroffs are friendly, helpful hosts who can direct you to any place you may wish to visit in the L.A. area. World travel is their hobby and they have maps, books, and a collection of articles to peruse. They can also help you choose from a variety of cuisines, whether you're looking for a fast food snack or an elegant meal. This refurbished Spanish-style home is on a residential street near a thriving commercial district. The B&B room is newly decorated, light, and airy. It features 1930's walnut furnishings with modern touches, a bright comforter, plush carpeting, and a folding writing shelf. Continental breakfast includes special treats in season from the back yard mini fruit orchard. Glendale is accessible to Universal and NBC studios, Pasadena Rose Bowl, Huntington Library, and other art galleries and botanical gardens. The Shroffs' home is also a good location for travelers who have business to conduct in this financially-oriented community.

No pets; TV; refrigerator; air cooler; convenient parking; train and bus pickup (Glendale); airport pickup (Burbank). Seventh night free for weekly stays.

Room	Bed	Bath	Entrance	Floor	Daily Rates S - D	(EP)
A	1D	Shd	Main	1	$25-$30	

Wildoaks Bed & Breakfast   **(619) 765-2168**
P.O. Box 1307, Julian, CA 92036
(Just west of town, off Highway 78)

It's hard to do justice to Julian in a few words. This picturesque mountain village is small in size, but large in authenticity. Once a booming gold mining town, it is now a popular weekend destination partway between the desert (Anzo Borrego) and the sea (at San Diego). Pat and Jim Svelmoe are among the friendly residents of Julian, and they enjoy providing a quiet rural spot for visitors who come to discover its treasures. Their home is on two acres of wild oaks and pines. A bedroom in the main house is carpeted and furnished in autumn tones. Guests may also use the large living room with fireplace and a screened-in porch. A separate cottage with a kitchen, bath, and large living/sleeping area provides spacious quarters for privacy-seekers. Paneled walls and oak furniture harmonize with the woodsy landscape. Whether you come to Julian for one of its seasonal festivities or just to escape the city and let your hair down, you'll appreciate the comfort and rest that Wildoaks has to offer.

No pets; no smoking in bedroom; child in cottage OK; no RV parking; full country breakfast; TV (A); extra single bed in cottage; dinner theater, antique shops, hiking, fishing, and picnic areas nearby. San Diego Wild Animal Park forty-five minutes away.

Room	Bed	Bath	Entrance	Floor	Daily Rates S - D	(EP)
A	1Q	Pvt	Main	1	$50	
B	2T or 1K	Pvt	Sep	1G	$65	($10)

Eagle's Landing   **(714) 336-2642**
Box 1510, Blue Jay, CA 92317
(In San Bernardino Mountains on west shore of lake)

This ingeniously designed home offers all the comfort and charm of a European mountain retreat, with many extra special touches. Finely crafted woodwork, plenty of view windows, and elements of Victorian styling make me think of a luxury tree house in a romantic Alpine setting. Each guest room is unique; all are private, quiet, and tastefully appointed with antiques, art, and handcrafted furnishings. Refreshments are served on a spacious deck or in the Hunt Room by a roaring fire, both with fantastic views of the lake. Breakfast at Eagle's Landing is a memorable event in the "Top of the Tower." Hosts Dorothy and Jack Stone provide unparalleled hospitality and attention to detail. In every respect, Eagle's Landing is a masterpiece.

No pets or children; smoking on decks only; TV in Hunt Room; kitchen privileges by arrangement; Room A has private deck; Room D is a 900-square-foot suite with fireplace, queen bed, TV, stereo, king sofa bed, and expansive lake view; boutique shopping, ice skating, fine dining, and quaint towns of Blue Jay and Arrowhead Village nearby. Brochure available.

Room	Bed	Bath	Entrance	Floor	Daily Rates S - D	(EP)
A	1Q	Pvt	Sep	3	$65	
B	1K	Pvt	Main	3	$55	
C	1K	Pvt	Main	2	$60	
D	1Q	Pvt	Sep	2	$85	($10)

Salisbury House   **(213) 737-7817**
2273 West 20th Street, Los Angeles, CA 90018
(Near Santa Monica Freeway and Western Avenue)

Experience a cozy kind of luxury at Salisbury House, the first accommodation of its kind in L.A. Here you'll find all the amenities of a manor house in the country, yet you'll be only minutes from downtown and major freeways. This turn-of-the-century California Craftsman home is large and solid. An expert restoration job has left its original integrity intact. Graciously proportioned rooms are exquisitely furnished with antiques and collectibles. Colors, fabrics, and nostalgia pieces are imaginatively combined to give each room a distinct personality. The total effect is enchanting. The generous breakfasts served here are superb, the hospitality boundless. Hosts Kathleen and Bill invite you to treat yourself to the many charms of Salisbury House. I can't imagine a more relaxing or romantic in-town spot.

No pets; full breakfast; complimentary wine; Room A has a sink; D is the 600-square-foot Attic Suite; E is the Sun Room Suite. Brochure available. Inquire about weekly and monthly rates. **KNIGHTTIME PUBLICATIONS SPECIAL RATE: 10% discount with this book.

Room	Bed	Bath	Entrance	Floor	Daily Rates S - D	(EP)
A	1Q	Pvt	Main	2	$55-$60	
B	1Q	Shd*	Main	2	$45-$50	
C	1Q	Shd*	Main	2	$45-$50	
D	1T & 1Q	Pvt	Main	3	$60-$65	($10)
E	2T & 1D	Pvt	Main	2	$60-$65	($10)

Terrace Manor   **(213) 381-1478**
1353 Alvarado Terrace, Los Angeles, CA 90006
(Downtown L.A., near Convention Center)

Amid the rapidly changing, fast-paced world of downtown Los Angeles, there is a little spot where time stands still. On Alvarado Terrace, a crescent of stately, historic homes faces a small park. Among them is Terrace Manor, a three-story Tudor-style home restored as a bed and breakfast establishment by hosts Sandy and Shirley Spillman. Built in 1902 for the owner of a glass factory, the home retains its original leaded and stained-glass windows. Rich, polished woodwork and bold colors give the interior an elegant warmth. A gallery of artwork adorns the walls. Choosing among the guest rooms is difficult. Each has a theme carried out in meticulous detail by period furnishings and unique collectibles. Whether you're soaking in a clawfoot tub, socializing in the library, or watching the world go by from the front porch swing, Terrace Manor takes you back to the genteel living of the prosperous, early Angelinos.

No pets or smoking; older children OK; full breakfast; afternoon refreshments; guest passes to Hollywood's Magic Castle where host performs and serves on board of directors; some Spanish spoken; secured parking; public transportation and airport connections. Room D is the Sun Room Suite. Brochure available. **KNIGHTTIME PUBLICATIONS SPECIAL RATE: 10% discount on Rooms D and E with this book.

Room	Bed	Bath	Entrance	Floor	Daily Rates S - D	(EP)
A	1D	Pvt	Main	2	$45-$55	
B	1D	Pvt	Main	2	$55-$65	
C	1Q	Pvt	Main	2	$65-$75	
D	1T & 1Q	Pvt	Main	2	$75-$85	($10)
E	1K	Pvt	Main	2	$75-$85	

Jim & Lila Sholes   **(805) 985-0434**
5223 Terramar Way, Oxnard, CA 93030
(Just north of Channel Islands Harbor)

   For anyone who hasn't discovered the shores of Oxnard, a getaway to this seaside community will be a great surprise. It's quiet and relatively uncrowded, with miles of lovely beach to walk on, good restaurants, and the headquarters of Channel Islands National Park. The home of Lila and Jim Sholes is just steps from the beach. Available to guests are two private bedrooms and a bath on the lower level; hosts serve breakfast upstairs in the living room or on the deck. During the day you may want to take the bikes out exploring, spend leisurely hours on the beach, go deep sea fishing, or learn about the Channel Islands. And in the evening you can soak away any last traces of tension in the enclosed garden spa. Whether you're making a brief escape from the city or a more extended visit, the relaxed hospitality of this B&B home will make you feel like you've really had a vacation.
   Two dogs in residence; no pets or smoking; spa; four bicycles; deep sea, surf, or pier fishing close by; tennis and sailing available; airport pickup (Ventura County).

Room	Bed	Bath	Entrance	Floor	Daily Rates S - D	(EP)
A	1Q	Shd*	Main	1G	$30-$35	
B	1Q	Shd*	Main	1G	$30-$35	

Bed & Breakfast in Mission Valley   **(619) 283-5146**
Box 100, 4102 30th Street, San Diego, CA 92104
(Above Hotel Circle)

You couldn't ask for a more central location than this Mission Valley home; the main attractions of San Diego are only minutes away. Lee Grace should write a book on the fine points of gracious hospitality. Her guests always come away with high praise for the cuisine, amenities, and comfortable lodgings at her B&B. The lower level of the house (a bedroom, bath, and sitting room) can accommodate up to four people and offers extra privacy. Add to all this an outstanding view of Mission Bay from the main floor, and you have an unbeatable combination.

No pets or RV parking; families welcome; afternoon refreshments; TV; laundry privileges; sitting room has queen-sized sofa bed; charge is $55 if both beds are used; $60 for four people.

Room	Bed	Bath	Entrance	Floor	Daily Rates S - D	(EP)
A	1Q	Pvt	Main	LL	$35-$45	

The Cottage   **(619) 299-1564**
P.O. Box 3292, San Diego, CA 92103
(Hillcrest area, near Balboa Park)

   The Hillcrest area is characterized by old homes and undeveloped canyons, offering an unhurried, isolated atmosphere. Conveniently located on a quiet cul-de-sac, this private cottage recreates the feeling of a Victorian country home. It is furnished with beautiful antiques, including such pieces as an oak pump organ and an old-time coffee grinder that still works. The accommodation includes a living room, bedroom, bath, and fully equipped kitchen; each is uncommonly charming. Your hosts, Bob and Carol Emerick, have thought of everything a traveler might need while in residence, and their vast collection of information about the area is yours to peruse (history, architecture, menus, maps, directions, etc.). If ever a place could inspire affection, The Cottage does just that. You may find yourself returning sooner than you think.
   TV; woodstove; kitchen; good public transportation.

Room	Bed	Bath	Entrance	Floor	Daily Rates S - D	(EP)
A	1T & 1K	Pvt	Sep	1	$40-$45	($5)

Barbara Farrell   **(619) 453-2982**
P.O. Box 12253, LaJolla, CA 92037-0620
(In San Diego, near LaJolla)

To be a guest at Barbara Farrell's townhouse is to have the best of San Diego at your fingertips. Barbara is a travel agent, a tour guide, a supporter of the symphony and the arts, and an avid world traveler. She is thoroughly familiar with the unique and exciting aspects of the area and is happy to share them with visitors. Nearest her home is LaJolla; she seems to know every nook and cranny of this jewel of a town. Guest quarters consist of a large, sunny upstairs bedroom with a private bath. It's attractively decorated in shades of blue and holds some of the special objects Barbara has found in her travels. Breakfast is usually served on the patio, which is surrounded by luxuriant foliage. For comfort, convenience, and insightful tips, Barbara's townhouse is just the ticket.

No pets, children, or smoking; TV; swimming pool, Jacuzzi, and tennis courts in complex; French spoken. Women and couples only. Early morning or evening calls best.

Room	Bed	Bath	Entrance	Floor	Daily Rates S - D	(EP)
A	1D	Pvt	Main	2	$38-$45	

Homecoming Bed & Breakfast   **(619) 583-3766**
4343 Lerida Drive, San Diego, CA 92115
(Near SDSU, south of I-8 at College Avenue Exit)

    Joy Reeder's contemporary home is in a quiet family neighborhood two miles from the state university campus. It is set on a sloping lot with a view and has three descending levels; the second is used for B&B guests. There's a bedroom, bath, and a smaller room with a twin bed. Accommodations are clean, light, and cheerful. You can be assured of a warm welcome, a good night's rest, and a satisfying breakfast at Homecoming B&B.
    No pets, smoking, small children, or RV parking; full breakfast; charge is $40 if both beds used for two guests.

Room	Bed	Bath	Entrance	Floor	Daily Rates S - D	(EP)
A	1T & 1D	Pvt	Sep	LL	$30-$35	($10)

Montana House   **(619) 268-8617**
8809 Polland Avenue, San Diego, CA 92123
(Just north of I-8 and east of I-805, Murray Ridge Exit)

Montana House is in a quiet residential area with quick access to downtown, beaches, the zoo, and Mission Bay. Hosts Jean and Larry Crawford, world travelers themselves, enjoy acquainting people with the diversity of attractions in and around San Diego. (Larry will even escort you by club coach to old Mexico or on a tour around town—free!) Jean hails from Montana and Larry from County Armagh, Ireland. Their home offers three guest rooms, all cool, clean, and comfortable. A large living room with a stone fireplace looks out upon a beautiful patio featuring an enormous Jacuzzi, a boon to the traveler at the end of an action-packed day. At Montana House, you'll find bed and breakfast in the old tradition: strangers turn into friends before they know it!

No pets; no children under eight; TV in each room and living room; kitchen privileges; spa; tours by arrangement; two private baths usually available; airport pickup (Lindbergh, Montgomery). Brochure available.

Room	Bed	Bath	Entrance	Floor	Daily Rates S - D (EP)
A	1D	Pvt	Main	1G	$30-$40
B	1D	Shd*	Main	1G	$30-$40
C	2T	Shd*	Main	1G	$30-$40

The Quiet Quail   **(619) 487-1037**
12326 Nacido Drive, San Diego, CA 92128
(In Rancho Bernardo)

With so many sunny days in Rancho Bernardo, the scenery is usually vibrant with color—red rooftops, deep blue skies, and bright green golf courses. The Quiet Quail is the home of Norma Hannah, a retired librarian who enjoys living in a newer residential neighborhood that's convenient and great for walking. She offers B&B guests the lovely master bedroom and bath, with sliding glass doors to a patio and secluded garden. Walls throughout the house display the landscape paintings of early California artists. Norma prides herself on her ability to please guests with her cooking, good FM music, and arrangements for anything from bridge to sports to dining. At The Quiet Quail, you can enjoy all the comforts of home in the resort atmosphere of sunny Rancho Bernardo.

No pets or children; smoking on patio; full breakfast; remote control TV in room; AC; laundry and limited kitchen privileges; swimming, golf, and tennis nearby. 10% discount after ten days.

Room	Bed	Bath	Entrance	Floor	Daily Rates S - D	(EP)
A	2T or 1K	Pvt	Main	1G	$30-$45	

The Craftsman   **(714) 558-1067**
1711 North Bush Street, Santa Ana, CA 92706
(Two blocks west of Santa Ana Freeway)

    Phil and Irene Chinn's Craftsman-style home was built in 1910. Each room has been refurbished to impart the flavor of the era using American oak and Danish antiques. Staying in this handsomely restored home puts you close to many local attractions, including Disneyland, Knott's Berry Farm, Newport Beach, and Bowers Museum. Your cordial hosts will help you choose from the profusion of fine restaurants and places to shop in the area. Though most people who visit The Craftsman arrive by car, it is also easy to reach by plane, train, or bus. The Chinns are glad to share their convenient location and lovely home with travelers.

    No pets; full breakfast; TV; kitchen privileges by arrangement; parks nearby; extra meals optional; airport pickup at extra charge (John Wayne-Orange County).

Room	Bed	Bath	Entrance	Floor	Daily Rates S - D	(EP)
A	1D	Shd*	Main	2	$35-$40	
B	1D	Shd*	Main	2	$35-$40	

The Cottage   **(805) 682-4997**
840 Mission Canyon Road, Santa Barbara, CA 93105
(Near Mission Santa Barbara)

Ray and Sylvia Byers offer the private guest cottage behind their home as a B&B accommodation. It is set among ancient trees and lush foliage, allowing only the songs of birds to awaken you each morning. The interior is paneled and nicely decorated in warm golds and browns. The cottage consists of a living room with a skylight, a bedroom, a bath, and a kitchenette with a refrigerator, but no facilities for cooking. In addition to the guest cottage, a spacious suite in the main house (B) will be available for B&B during most of the year. It too offers complete privacy and a refrigerator for guests. Within walking distance, Mission Santa Barbara and the botanical gardens are popular places to visit. Your hosts know the best beaches to send you to and the right restaurant for any occasion. For a homey feeling, extra privacy, and a convenient location, you can't go wrong with The Cottage.

Two dogs in residence; no pets or smoking; TV in each unit; German spoken. Two-night minimum on weekends and April-September; extra charge for one-night stays (cottage, $10; suite, $5); discount for more than three days and to former guests.

Room	Bed	Bath	Entrance	Floor	Daily Rates S - D	(EP)
A	1D	Pvt	Sep	1	$45-$55	($5)
B	1D & 3T	Pvt	Sep	1	$35-$40	($5)

Frank & Greta Hansen   **(805) 969-1365**
807 Cima Linda Lane, Montecito, CA 93108
(In hills overlooking Santa Barbara)

The view from the Hansens' elegant home is simply intoxicating. Whether you're sunbathing by the pool or ensconced in your comfortable room, the expanse of sea and sky is yours to behold. Guests may choose either a first-floor bedroom that opens to the patio/pool or an upstairs bedroom with a private sitting room. Each is tastefully appointed with decorator fabrics and wallcoverings. As a guest of the Hansens, you'll have luxurious accommodations, an incredible view, and a location that's only minutes from beaches and downtown Santa Barbara. I can see why many travelers find the combination irresistible.

Two dogs in residence; no children; TV and phone in each room; kitchen privileges by arrangement; swimming pool with Jacuzzi; airport pickup (Santa Barbara). Rates are $10 less after Labor Day until Memorial Day; $60 midweek rate with two-night minimum.

Room	Bed	Bath	Entrance	Floor	Daily Rates S - D	(EP)
A	1Q	Pvt	Main	1	$75	
B	1D	Pvt	Main	2	$75	

Marie Miller   **(805) 569-1914**
435 East Pedregosa, Santa Barbara, CA 93103
(Two blocks from Mission Santa Barbara)

    Marie Miller's Craftsman-style home was built in 1895. Mature shade trees surround the house, which has two commodious guest rooms with fireplaces. The tone here is calm and casual. Much of what you'll want to see and do in Santa Barbara is quite close at hand. A short walk takes you to the Mission, the Museum of Natural History, beautiful parks, and downtown. The wharf and beach are about ten minutes away by bicycle. Make your plans over a leisurely breakfast on the sunporch or patio. With a little luck, the rest of the day will just fall into place.

    Dog in residence; no pets; sundeck adjoins both rooms. Rates $5 less September-May; $5 per day less for five days or more.

Room	Bed	Bath	Entrance	Floor	Daily Rates S - D	(EP)
A	1Q	Shd*	Main	2	$45	
B	1T & 1Q	Shd*	Main	2	$45	($10)

Ocean View House
(805) 966-6659

P.O. Box 20065, Santa Barbara, CA 93102
(Three blocks from the ocean)

Bill and Carolyn Canfield have an attractive guest suite in their home. It has a bedroom, bath, and adjoining paneled den with a sofa bed and a private entrance. A complimentary drink and a generous Continental breakfast are served on the patio, a good vantage point for viewing sailboats and the Channel Islands with a background of vivid blue. Close by are beaches and lovely Shoreline Drive, a popular place for joggers, skaters, cyclists, and sightseers. The harbor and downtown Santa Barbara are within three miles. The playhouse in the back yard is a big favorite with children. If you need a relaxing spot that the whole family can appreciate, Ocean View House has all the necessary ingredients.

Dog and cat in residence; smoking on patio preferred; TV; pickup at bus or train station. Two-night minimum on weekends; $10 charge per person for using den sofa bed; $10 extra charge for one-night stays.

Room	Bed	Bath	Entrance	Floor	Daily Rates S - D	(EP)
A	1Q	Pvt	Sep	1G	$35-$40	

Valli's View   **(805) 969-1272**
340 North Sierra Vista, Montecito, CA 93108
(Foothills of Montecito)

    Valerie Buckley has fashioned the house of her dreams on the site where her earlier home stood. It burned in the big fire of 1977, though no hint of that event remains. She has reason to be proud: Valli's View is a beauty inside and out. Its ambiance of tranquility and comfort will soothe even the most frazzled nerves. There's a variety of places to relax outdoors—a spacious patio with lounge chairs, a porch swing, or a deck with a view of the mountains. In the evening, it's a pleasure to sit in the living room around the grand piano and fireplace. Guest quarters are at the far end of the house, affording added privacy. Soft-colored fabrics, rich carpeting, and antique oak pieces enhance the charming decor. Valerie offers a choice of tempting breakfasts (using seasonal fruits and vegetables from the garden) which she'll serve to you in bed, on the patio, or by the fireplace. As guest at Valli's View, you'll feel that your every need has been anticipated—a satisfying experience indeed.

    No indoor pets or smoking; full breakfast; TV; airport pickup (Santa Barbara). For stays of six days, the sixth is free.

Room	Bed	Bath	Entrance	Floor	Daily Rates S - D	(EP)
A	1D	Pvt	Main	1G	$50	

El Ranchito
1451 Alamo Pintado, Solvang, CA 93463
(Between Solvang and Ballard)

(805) 688-9517
or 688-9360

The Santa Ynez Valley is gaining well deserved fame as the Wine Country of the South, and the Danish community of Solvang attracts a multitude of visitors year-round. El Ranchito, home of Don and Joan Speirs, offers a priceless opportunity to bask in the picturesque countryside just outside of Solvang. The architecture and total feeling are strongly old-world Mediterranean. Two exquisite guest houses (Villa Fiore and Villa Amore) on the property were constructed using old French windows and antiques in keeping with the recently restored main house. Both have balconies with wonderful views. The Speirs family raises and breeds llamas, endearing animals with movie stars' names. There's an inviting pond with a waterfall for swimming. The grounds are dotted with fruit trees and grape vines, while a cottage garden and a bed of roses thrive near the house. The setting, the view, and the charm of El Ranchito are truly beyond compare.

Various outdoor animals are raised; no pets, children, smoking, or RV parking; full breakfast; refreshments; TV; airport pickup (Santa Ynez).

Room	Bed	Bath	Entrance	Floor	Daily Rates S - D	(EP)
A	2T or 1K	Pvt	Sep	2	$85	
B	1Q	Pvt	Sep	1	$85	

Mary & George Hendrick   **(818) 919-2125**
2124 East Merced Avenue, West Covina, CA 91791
(Between Freeways 60 and 10, Azusa Exit)

The Hendricks' home in West Covina will give you a real taste of the California lifestyle. The large, rambling house was once photographed inside and out by *Life* magazine. It has a gorgeous deck area with a swimming pool, a separate Jacuzzi, and good outdoor furniture. The master suite (D), a guest room with rainbow motif (B), and one of the living rooms face the deck. There's plenty of space to relax here, and the Hendricks' laid-back style will put you at ease. Genial conversationalists and inveterate travelers, Mary and George can provide all manner of help to people unfamiliar with the area. They'll direct you to special undiscovered spots or to the more popular attractions. Their home is centrally located for visiting Disneyland, L.A., mountains, and desert. If you don't catch some of the California spirit at the Hendricks', consider yourself immune.

No pets; school-age children welcome; refreshments; TV; AC; two living rooms with fireplaces; swimming pool; Jacuzzi; extra meals optional (rave reviews from guests!); good airport connections. Suite (D) only available for stays of three days or longer. A beach home at Ensenada and a cottage on Prudence Island, Rhode Island, available for rental or B&B; inquiries welcome.

Room	Bed	Bath	Entrance	Floor	Daily Rates S - D	(EP)
A	2T	Shd*	Main	1G	$35	
B	1D	Shd*	Main	1G	$30	
C	1T	Shd*	Main	1G	$25	
D	1K	Pvt	Main	1G	$40	

Pretzel-Haus   **(818) 919-8777**
1418 Hollencrest Drive, West Covina, CA 91791
(Between Freeways 60 and 10, Azusa Exit)

Although the Pretzliks' home is in a populated area near freeways and the buzz of modern life, it is an island of tranquility. The lovely ranch-style home is situated below street level. Gently rolling hills extend behind the house, and there are no neighbors close by. In the beautifully landscaped yard, guests may picnic or use the spa under a redwood gazebo. Views of snow-capped Mount Baldy and the San Gabriel Mountains can sometimes be seen in the distance. The Pretzliks' German heritage is evident throughout the house. Furnishings, art, and needlework are interesting reminders of their native land. Busy travelers will find the old-world atmosphere a haven of peace and quiet.

Two dogs on premises; no pets; child over five OK; TV; AC; kitchen privileges by arrangement; extra bed; spa; extra meals optional; German, French, and some Swedish and Spanish spoken. Large parties might consider the Pretzel-Haus and the Hendricks' home for lodging in close proximity. Suite (B) available only for stays of three days or longer.

Room	Bed	Bath	Entrance	Floor	Daily Rates S - D	(EP)
A	1D	Shd	Main	1G	$30	
B	1K	Pvt	Main	1G	$45	

Oregon

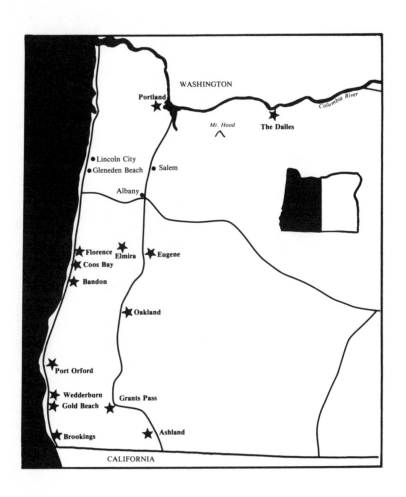

From silken beaches to icy peaks to high desert plateaus to crumbled lava fields, Oregon is a state rich in contrasts. To travel Oregon is to experience both the astonishing power and the delicate beauty of nature.

The Oregon Coast alone is a dramatic confrontation of ocean, beach, and forest. To the west is the longest unimpeded expanse of open ocean on earth—neither islands nor reefs stand between Oregon and the beaches of Japan, six thousand miles away. To the east loom the mountains of the Coast Range, which rose gradually in a series of thunderous, continuous volcanic eruptions some forty million years ago. In between are the glorious beaches, some stretching for as many as ten miles, with jagged rocks dotting the surf like shaggy beasts looking for a home, spindrift blowing up from the restless waves, and cypress trees clutching at the wind with their tentacle-like branches. Highway 101 is a cliff-hanger, riding the tan shoulders of mountains up to two thousand feet above the water.

Oregon's coastline is by law "forever free," which means noncommercial and open to the public. There is a state park every five miles or so. In addition to spectacular scenery, fishing is the main attraction. Try some kaboodle fishing from the rocks (so called because on a good day you can catch "the whole kit and kaboodle") or rent a crab pot at one of the small towns, such as Gold Beach or Bandon, for some luscious Dungeness crab.

Gold Beach, at the mouth of the renowned Rogue River, is a favorite spot for the spring and fall runs of Chinook salmon and steelhead trout. If you're a sightseer, you might want to take a jet boat excursion through the Rogue's whitewater rapids. You can also explore this wilderness by foot, by car, or on horseback.

Further north lie some of the highest coastal dunes in the world, rising hundreds of feet above the water, sometimes burying whole spruce pine forests. For forty-five miles, the sandy hills and hollows of the Oregon Dunes National Recreational Area drift and change shape daily.

Roughly paralleling the coast, from its midpoint north, is Oregon's lush heartland, the Willamette Valley. The Eugene-Springfield area occupies its southerly pocket, only sixty miles from the coast.

Eugene, cradled in natural beauty, has all the advantages of a city— museums, shops, cultural and entertainment opportunities, and a major university—yet is also the gateway to unlimited outdoor recreation. Just a few miles to the west, near Elmira, the Fern River Reservoir invites boating, fishing, and swimming. To the east is the McKenzie River, famous for its scenery and watersports like kayaking. South is the Bohemia mining country, a primitive region of unfettered mountain streams, wildlife, shadowy gorges, cleavered scarps, and jagged peaks. You can navigate the narrow dirt roads yourself or take a landrover tour in search of ghost towns and lost mines.

The Willamette River flows generally north-south for the length of the valley, dissecting a city at one point, cutting through rolling hills or thick forests at another. You can go cruising down the river on a float trip or try some "shunpiking," a word that means motoring the backroads. Here classic covered bridges, pastoral picnic sites, and small towns whose streets are lined with well-preserved historic buildings will take you back in time.

The Willamette flows right through the center of Portland, where it joins the mighty Columbia, creating a waterfront setting for the city's skyline. Within sixty miles is the famous Columbia Gorge/ Mount Hood area. The Gorge is the scene of sparkling waterfalls plunging over huge cliffs formed by the Columbia River as it cuts its path through the Cascade Mountain Range, the stony and spectacular backbone of the state. Toward the eastern end is the towering Mount Hood, the only peak in North America to offer year-round downhill skiing. With its gentle southern slope, Mount Hood is the most climbed mountain in the nation.

A major volcanic attraction is Crater Lake National Park, high in the southern Cascades. The lake, the deepest in the United States, was formed when Mount Mazama blew its top more than six thousand years ago and collapsed into its own crater, forming a caldern six miles across. The exceptionally clear and brilliant water, looking like melted sapphires, is the result of accumulated snowmelt.

South of Crater Lake, nestled between the Cascades and the Coast Range is a delightful contrast of culture and natural beauty. In the country surrounding Ashland, you can enjoy Shakespeare, classical concerts, Gold Rush history, whitewater rafting, hiking, and skiing. Ashland's famous outdoor Shakespeare Festival is held from June through September, but the regular season runs from February through October. Nearby Jacksonville, a National Historic Landmark, preserves the Gold Rush atmosphere of the 1850's. Eighty homes and buildings have been restored, and you can ride a stagecoach in the Pioneer Village district. Jacksonville hosts the Peter Britt Music and Arts Festival in August for classical music lovers. Concerts for bluegrass and jazz fans are enjoyed here, too.

Rushing rivers, rugged peaks, cold blue lakes, stark and lovely deserts, unspoiled beaches. . .and the peace and quiet in which to enjoy it. Some people say Oregon has it all.

The Miners Addition   **(503) 482-0562**
737 Siskiyou Boulevard, Ashland, OR 97520
(Walking distance to downtown and theaters)

Carolyn Morris invites you to "come and enjoy a bit of Ashland history. Stay at The Miners Addition, a historic home built in 1900 and dedicated to the gold miners of Jackson County." You can't miss it: an old ore car occupies a prominent position in the front yard. Two upstairs guest rooms are named for local mines, the Sterling and the Maltern. Both have painted floors, rag rugs, antique quilts, and a cozy, friendly feeling. Carolyn's hearty breakfasts often include sourdough pancakes, the house specialty. A lovely back yard is inviting for guests who wish to relax in the garden summerhouse. Theaters, shops, and restaurants await you at the end of a six-block stroll along the boulevard. The gold miners would probably be surprised at the Ashland of today. I'm certain they'd be pleased that their memory lives on at The Miners Addition.

No pets or smoking; children over five welcome; full breakfast; AC; airport pickup (Ashland, or Medford at a nominal charge). Brochure available. Off-season rates November-January.

Room	Bed	Bath	Entrance	Floor	Daily Rates S - D	(EP)
A	1T & 1Q	Pvt	Main	2	$50-$60	($10)
B	1T & 1D	Pvt	Main	2	$50-$60	($10)

Parkside Cottage & Suite   **(503) 482-2320**
P.O. Box 721, Ashland, OR 97520
(171 Granite Street, adjacent to Lithia Park)

Susan and Rod Reid offer B&B accommodations in the fully furnished 1914 cottage (A) beside their home. In addition to the cottage, a full guest suite (B) inside the main house is now available. Each has its own entrance and kitchenette; the suite has a living room and a front porch with a swing. From the Reids', it's a five-minute walk through beautiful Lithia Park to the Shakespearean theaters and plaza. Tennis courts and jogging trails in Lithia Park, plus other recreational and cultural opportunities in the area surrounding Ashland, make the Parkside Cottage and Suite a spot for year-round enjoyment.

No pets. Inquire about weekly rates.

Room	Bed	Bath	Entrance	Floor	Daily Rates S - D	(EP)
A	1Q	Pvt	Sep	1	$35	
B	1Q	Pvt	Sep	1	$45	

Spindrift Bed & Breakfast   **(503) 347-2275**
2990 Beach Loop Road, Bandon, OR 97411
(Overlooking ocean)

Ocean lovers, rejoice! No more straining for a glimpse of blue from
"ocean front" rooms. Witness the breathtaking beauty of the Oregon Coast
at Spindrift B&B. This lovely home is perched on a bluff just forty feet above
a long, sandy beach that is framed by massive offshore rock formations. Un-
interrupted vistas are yours from floor-to-ceiling windows in the common
room, the large deck with direct beach access, or one of the attractive guest
rooms (A). You'll be able to watch the ever-changing surf, sea animals,
glorious sunsets, or the approach of spectacular storms. There are two accommodations for guests. The Seaview has a magnificent view, a feeling of openness, a fireplace, and French doors leading to the deck (with private ramp entrance). The Surfsound, smaller but still quite appealing, has extra comfortable twin beds. The common room has a vaulted, beamed ceiling, a fireplace,
and a view that guests enjoy while visiting with hosts Don and Robbie Smith.
Breakfast at Spindrift is a real feast, so bring a hearty appetite. The Smiths offer their friendship, but they can also provide relaxing privacy if that is what
you need.

Full breakfast; bridge players welcome; airport pickup at extra charge
(North Bend). Brochure available. Ask about family rates.

Room	Bed	Bath	Entrance	Floor	Daily Rates S - D	(EP)
A	1Q	Pvt	Main	1G	$55-$60	
B	2T	Pvt	Main	1G	$40-$45	

Sea Dreamer Bed & Breakfast   **(503) 469-6629**
P.O. Box 1840, Brookings, OR 97415
(Three miles north of California border, just off U.S. 101)

Judy and Bob Blair named the Sea Dreamer after their sailboat, a thirty-foot Bahama Islander docked at the Port of Brookings. Not surprisingly, there's a nautical theme to their home and, best of all, a gorgeous view past lily fields down to the wide open sea. Built in 1912 of redwood, the two-story, blue home is set on spacious grounds of lawn, trees, and flowers. Becky, the resident sheep, grazes close by. There are four tastefully appointed guest rooms, three with ocean views. Refreshments are served in the living room around sunset time, and a fire is lit in the hearth whenever a chill sets in. As the Blairs can tell you, there is no shortage of things to do along this stretch of coastline. Let the Sea Dreamer add a touch of romance to your seaside vacation.

No pets, children, or smoking; full breakfast; bridal suite. Brochure available.

Room	Bed	Bath	Entrance	Floor	Daily Rates S - D	(EP)
A	1D	Pvt	Main	1	$50-$55	
B	1Q	Pvt	Main	2	$50-$55	
C	1Q	Shd*	Main	2	$45-$50	
D	2T	Shd*	Main	2	$40-$45	

This Olde House   (503) 267-5224
202 Alder Street, Coos Bay, OR 97420
(Just off U.S. 101 at North Second Street)

This stately house on the hill is every inch a lady. She is pale blue trimmed in white, with all her grandeur still intact. Ed and Jean Mosieur moved from Monterey to Coos Bay, trading one coastal location for another. Things are calmer in Coos Bay, slower paced. Renovations and furnishings have made the Mosieurs' new old home a gracious, inviting place for guests to enjoy a special brand of hospitality. There are four generously proportioned guest rooms, three with a bay view and one with a canopied bed. A short drive takes you to one of my favorite parts of the Oregon coast, the fishing village of Charleston (great for buying fresh and smoked fish) and three adjacent state parks that are worth a special trip: Sunset Bay, Shore Acres, and Cape Arago. Ed, Jean, and Brice are sure to make your stop in Coos Bay a memorable one.

No pets or smoking; no children under forty-three (Jean's humor).

Room	Bed	Bath	Entrance	Floor	Daily Rates S - D	(EP)
A	1K	Pvt	Main	2	$55	($10)
B	1K	Shd*	Main	2	$47	($10)
C	1K	Shd*	Main	2	$47	($10)
D	1Q	Shd*	Main	2	$47	($10)

Bigelow Bed & Breakfast   **(503) 296-3081**
308 East Fourth Street, The Dalles, OR 97058
(Center of town at 606 Washington Street)

Even though Bigelow Bed & Breakfast is in The Dalles' downtown area, it is secluded by trees and very quiet. The 1862 Victorian home has two upstairs bedrooms for guests. They are done in pastel colors and delicate prints. The back room (A) faces east and has a private deck that catches the morning sun. The front room (B) has a waterbed and a woodstove. A bathroom with a clawfoot tub is shared by both. Host Jan Mlnarik features breakfast items from her nearby deli. She knows The Dalles well and can guide you to a historic walking tour, recreational activities along the Columbia River Gorge, climbs of Mount Hood, bicycle loops, and various seasonal events. Being a private pilot herself, she enjoys catering to those who fly into the airport across the river. The area has an interesting past and an array of outdoor attractions to delight the traveler.

Dog in residence; no pets or RV parking; smoking outside only; airport pickup (Dallesport, WA). Other B&B referrals for The Dalles available.

Room	Bed	Bath	Entrance	Floor	Daily Rates S - D	(EP)
A	1D	Shd	Main	2	$30-$35	
B	1Q	Shd	Main	2	$30-$35	

McGillivrays' Log Home Bed & Breakfast　　　　　**(503) 935-3564**
88680 Evers Road, Elmira, OR 97437
(Off Highway 126, west of Eugene enroute to Florence and coast)

　　　The McGillivrays' unique, built-from-scratch log home is well-suited to its environment: five acres mostly covered with pine and fir trees. Much care and hard work went into the construction of the home, which combines the best of the past with the comforts of today. Throughout the interior, there is handcrafted woodwork displaying a variety of different woods. One guest room (A) with private bath is on the ground floor. An impressive stairway of half-logs leads to a balcony which overlooks the living and dining areas. Doors lead from the balcony to a spacious bedroom (B) with a bath and a small deck. Old-fashioned breakfasts are usually prepared on the antique, wood-burning cookstove in the dining room, a good place to linger over coffee and plan your day. Many people are understandably quite taken with the McGillivrays' log home, but I think a child guest summed it up best when he asked them, "You mean you get to live here *all* the time?"

　　　No pets; families welcome; smoking on covered porches only; TV; AC; extra beds; crib; winery touring and tasting nearby (Forgeron Vineyards); outdoor recreation at Fern Ridge Reservoir; wheelchair access; airport pickup (Mahlon Sweet).

Room	Bed	Bath	Entrance	Floor	Daily Rates S - D	(EP)
A	1K	Pvt	Main	1G	$35-$40	
B	1K	Pvt	Main	2	$45-$50	

Griswolds' Bed & Breakfast　　　　　　　　　　**(503) 683-6294**
552 West Broadway, Eugene, OR 97401
(Five blocks from downtown area)

　　　The Griswolds' large, old family home is located on a tree-shaded street not far from downtown and city transit stops. Jogging and biking trails along the Willamette River are nine blocks away. The upstairs guest rooms are comfortably appointed with soft colors and homey furnishings. Coffee is on outside your door when you awaken, and the downstairs living room with fireplace is yours to enjoy at any time. At the Griswolds' you'll find an authentic home-away-from-home atmosphere. Many of their guests feel like members of the family by the time they leave; I'd say that's a pretty good measure of success.

　　　No pets; children welcome; no smoking upstairs; full breakfast; living room for guests; good public transportation. Children under five free. 10% discount for stays of one week or longer, October-February. Brochure available.

Room	Bed	Bath	Entrance	Floor	Daily Rates S - D	(EP)
A	1Q	Shd*	Main	2	$34-$39	($10)
B	1D	Shd*	Main	2	$30-$35	($10)

The House in the Woods   (503) 343-3234
814 Lorane Highway, Eugene, OR 97405
(SW Eugene, South Hills area)

The Lorane Highway is a thoroughfare for joggers and cyclists and a convenient route to downtown Eugene, three miles away. The House in the Woods is set back from the road, with a periphery of fir and oak trees, an abundance of azaleas and rhododendrons, and some formally landscaped open areas. Friendly wildlife still abounds on the two acres. Long-time residents Eunice and George Kjaer have restored their 1908 home to its original quiet elegance. There are hardwood floors with Oriental carpets, high ceilings, lots of windows, and three covered porches (one with a swing). A large, comfortable parlor is most pleasant for visiting, listening to music, or reading by the fireplace. Guest rooms are spacious and tastefully decorated. Parks, cultural events, outdoor recreation, and good restaurants can be pointed out by your versatile hosts, but the house and grounds are so peaceful and relaxing that you may be compelled to stay put.

No pets; children over twelve welcome; smoking on outside covered areas; full breakfast (Continental style for late risers); TV; piano; music library; airport pickup (Mahlon Sweet). Brochure available. Additional bedroom with twin bed and shared bath at $35 is available as an alternate choice.

Room	Bed	Bath	Entrance	Floor	Daily Rates S - D	(EP)
A	1Q	Pvt	Main	1	$38-$50	
B	1D	Shd	Main	2	$35-$45	

Shelley's Guest House   **(503) 683-2062**
1546 Charnelton Street, Eugene, OR 97401
(Walking distance to downtown and University of Oregon)

Lois and Bill Shelley have turned a simple little 1928 bungalow into a true work of art. No shortcuts were taken in the restoration and the result is something rare: total perfection. Gleaming woodwork and floors, traditional wallcoverings, brass accents, and selected antiques enhance the interior. There's comfortable seating around the living room fireplace and an extensive library to browse through. The upstairs is used exclusively by guests. A cozy sitting room with cable TV connects the Master Bedroom (A) and the Guest Room (B). Each is positively charming. A spacious bathroom with separate tub and tile shower can be shared or included as part of a Master Suite. Consideration for the convenience and comfort of guests is obvious throughout the house. For example, there's a lamp or light switch wherever you could possibly need one, plus many extra amenities. Breakfast features some delectable entrees. Elegance and personal service are hallmarks of the hospitality you'll find at Shelley's.

No pets; no children under twelve; smoking outside only; full breakfast; TV; deck; bicycles; public transportation; airport pickup (Mahlon Sweet). Master Suite with private bath and sitting room is $60 by arrangement.

Room	Bed	Bath	Entrance	Floor	Daily Rates S - D	(EP)
A	1Q	Shd*	Main	2	$40-$45	
B	1D	Shd*	Main	2	$30-$35	

Wheeler's Bed & Breakfast   **(503) 344-1366**
P.O. Box 8201, Coburg, OR 97401
(Off I-5, seven miles north of Eugene)

The beautiful Cascades surround this fertile valley where the McKenzie and the Willamette Rivers meet. Whether you're just passing through or staying long enough to explore a bit, Joe and Isabel Wheeler will be happy to share their comfortable home with you. Joe built the house himself, and B&B guests are sure to find it as livable as he and Isabel do. They offer two spacious, carpeted bedrooms upstairs which are separate enough from the rest of the house to assure complete privacy. A third bedroom for guests on the main floor is smaller, but comfy as can be. Coburg is a unique little farming community with antique stores and century-old homes. Just a short walk from the Wheelers' home, a fine meal can be yours at the renowned Coburg Inn (1877). Picturesque surroundings, a taste of history, and a gracious welcome await you at Wheeler's B&B.

Full breakfast; TV; living room for guests; airport pickup (Mahlon Sweet). Brochure available.

Room	Bed	Bath	Entrance	Floor	Daily Rates S - D	(EP)
A	2T	Shd*	Main	2	$25-$30	
B	1D	Shd*	Main	2	$25-$30	
C	1Q	Shd*	Main	1	$25-$30	

The Johnson House   **(503) 997-8000**
P.O. Box 1892, Florence, OR 97439
(216 Maple Street, Old Town Florence)

    The Johnson House, built in 1892, is the oldest house in Florence. Its structure and details are original, and the furnishings are so authentic that when I visited, I thought I'd stepped into a time warp. Hosts Jayne and Ron Fraese have made sure that all the elements of the decor "evoke the atmosphere of warm, plain living on the Oregon coast nearly a century ago." They have long been attracted to the coast and can point out some of its lesser-known wonders. Florence makes a good base for exploring the Oregon Dunes, attending the annual Rhododendron Festival, or visiting historical sites. Nature lovers are drawn to the area for its abundant wildlife and unspoiled beauty. What good fortune that The Johnson House has been restored and opened for lodging. Known as a "small family-style inn with cheerful rooms and hearty breakfasts," it's exactly what Florence needed.

    No pets; no children under twelve; smoking on porch; full breakfast; afternoon refreshments; French spoken; airport pickup (Florence). Rooms A-D share two baths. Brochure available.

Room	Bed	Bath	Entrance	Floor	Daily Rates S - D	(EP)
A	1D	Shd*	Main	2	$45	
B	1D	Shd*	Main	2	$45	($10)
C	1D	Shd*	Main	2	$45	($10)
D	1D	Shd*	Main	2	$45	
E	1D	Pvt	Main	1	$55	($10)

Endicott Gardens   **(503) 247-6513**
95768 Jerrys Flat Road, Gold Beach, OR 97444
(Four miles east of U.S. 101)

Endicott Gardens is the setting for a small nursery and the home of Stewart and Mary Endicott. Bed and breakfast accommodations have been constructed in a separate wing of the house, consisting of four bedrooms with private baths. Rooms C and D open to a deck that is blessed with a view of the forest and mountains. As one might imagine, the grounds are spectacular with flowers and shrubs. Breakfast on the deck is a delight, but in cool weather Mary presents hearty morning fare in the dining room while the nearby fireplace crackles and warms. Guests are provided with some thoughtful amenities, and the cordial climate set by your hosts is spiced with humor. Endicott Gardens offers the traveler all this, plus a chance to unwind in a quiet, natural environment.

No pets; full breakfast; TV available; Rogue River, ocean, and forest recreation nearby; airport pickup (Gold Beach). Brochure available. Garden wedding receptions by arrangement.

Room	Bed	Bath	Entrance	Floor	Daily Rates S - D	(EP)
A	2T	Pvt	Sep	1G	$35-$45	($10)
B	1Q	Pvt	Sep	1G	$35-$45	($10)
C	1T & 1Q	Pvt	Sep	1G	$35-$45	($10)
D	1Q	Pvt	Sep	1G	$35-$45	($10)

Wedderburn House   **(503) 247-6126**
P.O. Box 592, Wedderburn, OR 97491
(Thirty-seven miles from California border)

Wedderburn House, built in the 1890's, occupies a prime site overlooking the point where the Rogue River meets the sea. A popular choice for visitors is a ride by jet boat up the wild and scenic Rogue. Ocean and river fishing for salmon and steelhead tempts anglers to the limit. A half-mile walk to a jetty and beach can lead to hours of beachcombing, watching birds and sea lions, and gathering driftwood. Ken and Lea Leonard invite you to enjoy all this as their guest at Wedderburn House. After a full day's activities, and perhaps a hearty seafood dinner, you're welcome to join the Leonards around the fireplace in the living room. It's a virtual certainty that you'll sleep comfortably in the lovely, old-fashioned guest suite on the first floor—a perfect ending to a perfect day.

Dog in residence; children welcome; smoking outside only; no RV parking; TV; extra bedrooms upstairs; airport pickup (Gold Beach). *Open May 15-October 1.* Brochure available.

Room	Bed	Bath	Entrance	Floor	Daily Rates S - D (EP)
A	1D	Pvt	Main	1	$40

Lawnridge House   **(503) 479-5186**
1304 NW Lawnridge, Grants Pass, OR 97526
(One-half mile from I-5, Exit 58)

      Lawnridge is a tranquil, tree-lined street in a neighborhood of lovely older homes. Set on a shaded corner lot, Lawnridge House looks friendly and inviting. It has been recently restored with exquisite care. The tasteful interior is enhanced by coffered ceilings, lustrous woodwork and floors, and comfortable antique furnishings. Guest rooms are especially attractive; Room B is ideal for honeymooners or other romantics. There are shady, secluded porches and a small orchard in back. The overall effect is gracious and serene. Host Barbara Head features fresh salmon steaks with breakfast, an example of the impeccable quality you'll find at Lawnridge House.

      No pets or RV parking; smoking outside only; full breakfast; TV; VCR; AC; host suggests day trips from Grants Pass to Crater Lake, the Oregon Coast, Ashland, Jacksonville, Wolf Creek Tavern, Rogue River activities, Oregon Caves, wineries, ghost towns, and the Britt Music and Dance Festivals; Spanish, French, and German spoken; airport pickup (Josephine County, Medford). Brochure available. Lower rates off-season (mid-October to mid-May).

Room	Bed	Bath	Entrance	Floor	Daily Rates S - D	(EP)
A	1Q	Shd*	Main	2	$40-$45	
B	1K	Pvt	Main	2	$50-$55	

The Nicholson House   **(503) 479-5687**
1026 NW Prospect, Grants Pass, OR 97526   **or 479-0487**
(Almost a mile from I-5, Exit 58)

    The Nicholson House is a large, old country Victorian set on a peaceful, tree-covered estate. As you drive up the driveway, anticipation builds. When you walk through the front door, expectation turns to delight. The house is loaded with character. Dark, rich woodwork, rosy colors, and handsome antiques grace the light-bathed rooms. A private suite makes a romantic haven for guests. There is a sitting room with comfortable sofas and French doors leading to a bedroom with a beautiful brass and iron bed. A fire is often crackling in the hearth of each room. A private bath, entrance foyer, and secluded porch complete the guest accommodations. For your recreational pleasure, there is a large swimming pool and a tennis court. Guests have been known to change travel plans just so they can spend more time at The Nicholson House.

    Cat in residence; smoking on porch; full breakfast; fireplaces; swimming pool; tennis court; queen sofa bed available; French spoken. *Open May 15-October 15.*

Room	Bed	Bath	Entrance	Floor	Daily Rates S - D	(EP)
A	1Q	Pvt	Sep	1	$75	($10)

Pringle House   **(503) 459-5038**
P.O. Box 578, Oakland, OR 97462
(Two miles east of I-5; Seventh and Locust Streets)

      Pringle House stands on a rise at one end of the main street of Oakland, a quaint little town of 850 people that is on the National Register of Historic Places. The 1893 Queen Anne Victorian has been lovingly restored and decorated with turn-of-the-century style. Each of the upstairs guest rooms has a unique personality. Public rooms include a front parlor, a living room with a fireplace and winged-back chairs, and a dining room where coffee, tea, and juices are always available. But those are only the basics. It's Jim and Demay Pringle themselves who make their B&B truly one of a kind. Imagination and hard work have transformed this old house into a home of distinction and warmth. It is literally packed with nostalgic treasures, each with a history (or at least a story). There are countless discoveries to be made without even leaving the house. Only in museums have I seen more collections; Demay's dolls fill an entire room, floor to ceiling. The friendliness, the sense of fun, and the generous hospitality at Pringle House make it a place you'll remember with a smile.

      Two cats in residence; older children by arrangement; no pets; smoking on porches; full breakfast; robes provided; historic walking tour, a museum, and Tolly's Dinner House and Ice Cream Parlor nearby. Brochure available.

Room	Bed	Bath	Entrance	Floor	Daily Rates S - D	(EP)
A	1T & 1Q	Shd*	Main	2	$30-$35	($10)
B	1D	Shd*	Main	2	$30-$35	

Bed & Roses   (503) 254-3206
10170 SE Market Street, Portland, OR 97216
(Just off I-205, ten minutes from downtown and the airport)

An appropriate place to stay in the "City of Roses" is Wendy Ackerman's guest house, Bed & Roses. Her white Cape Cod home has blue shutters, a white picket fence, and a meticulously landscaped yard that includes beds of gorgeous roses. There is also a grape arbor where Wendy's nourishing, made-from-scratch breakfasts are sometimes enjoyed. The newly remodeled guest house is behind the main house. It has two large, beautifully furnished bedrooms with comfortable sitting areas. The shared bath and both bedrooms are entered from a hallway where shelves hold a diverse collection of reading matter. The sparkling clean guest quarters are outfitted with creature comforts to satisfy even the most particular traveler. Wendy is a busy registered nurse employed in the hospital across the street from her home, but she makes no compromises in the quality and service of her breakfasts, or in catering to the special needs of her guests.

No smoking, children under twelve, or pets; full breakfast; TV and clock radio in each room; jogging/exercise path across street; bike/walking path to Columbia River nearby. Brochure available. *Advance reservations essential.*

Room	Bed	Bath	Entrance	Floor	Daily Rates S - D	(EP)
A	1Q	Shd*	Sep	1G	$30-$35	
B	1T & 1D	Shd*	Sep	1G	$30-$35	($10)

Corbett House   **(503) 245-2580**
7533 SW Corbett Avenue, Portland, OR 97219
(Above John's Landing; three miles from city center)

The views alone would make Corbett House worth a visit. It's on a hill in a gracious old southwest Portland neighborhood that overlooks the Willamette River and the city, with Mount St. Helens and Mount Hood visible in the distance. To me, a sunrise from this vantage point had the impact of an unexpected gift from the gods. Sylvia Malagamba has achieved the exceptional in Corbett House. With sensitivity and artistic flair, she has created a place so aesthetically soothing that complete relaxation is virtually assured. Three guest rooms sharing two baths occupy the second floor, and each is highlighted by unique plants, books, and objects of art. A mildly exotic flavor prevails in the tastefully constructed decor, and there is soft music drifting through the house. In the morning, breakfast cuisine that matches the high quality of everything else at Corbett House is yours to savor.

No pets; no children under ten; smoking on porch, patio, or balcony only; small extra charge for more elaborate breakfast specialties; laundry privileges; patio; good shopping, restaurants, and public transportation nearby; limited Spanish and Italian spoken; good airport connections; Rooms B and C share a balcony. Brochure available. Major credit cards accepted. **KNIGHTTIME PUBLICATIONS SPECIAL RATE: 10% discount with this book.

Room	Bed	Bath	Entrance	Floor	Daily Rates S - D	(EP)
A	1D	Shd*	Main	2	$35-$40	
B	2T or 1K	Shd*	Main	2	$45-$50	
C	1Q	Shd*	Main	2	$45-$50	

Marcelle & John Tebo (503) 246-1839
5733 SW Dickinson, Portland, OR 97219
(Seven miles south of downtown Portland)

Whether you have business in Portland or you're taking a quick break enroute to someplace else, the Tebos' lovely Cape Cod home can be a restful stopping place. It's in an older residential neighborhood with plenty of trees and hardly any traffic. The upstairs can be closed off for guests, affording the utmost privacy. There are two pleasant bedrooms and a newly renovated bath. Antiques and traditional furniture are combined throughout the house. Marcelle tends a huge garden and serves delicious homemade jams and jellies with your full or Continental breakfast. This B&B home is an hour's drive from the beach or the mountains. It is just off the main route from Portland to the coast (Highways 99W and 18), which takes you through one of Oregon's major wine regions. It's a great place to begin or end a day of vineyard-hopping.

No pets or smoking; AC; public transportation (six blocks); some French spoken; airport pickup (Portland International).

Room	Bed	Bath	Entrance	Floor	Daily Rates S - D	(EP)
A	1D	Shd*	Main	2	$25-$30	
B	2T	Shd*	Main	2	$20-$35	

Madelaine's Bed & Breakfast   **(503) 332-4373**
P.O. Box 913, Port Orford, OR 97465
(735 8th Street at U.S. 101)

Madelaine's is a small country-style guest house with lots of personality. There's a comfortable parlor with an antique carousel horse above the fireplace and three delightful guest rooms. Calico print fabrics, brass and lace accents, aged wooden paneling, and colorful braided rugs punctuate the decor. The bathroom walls display a collection of old iron tools. It's just a short walk from Madelaine's to the beach, a movie theater, and a choice seafood restaurant. People arriving by bus or private plane could easily do without a car. Gwendolyn Guerin can be your guide to the wealth of outdoor wonders and seasonal events in the Port Orford area.

No pets; no smoking in bedrooms; TV on request; laundry privileges; airport pickup (Cape Blanco). Master Card, Visa, and Canadian currency accepted.

Room	Bed	Bath	Entrance	Floor	Daily Rates S - D	(EP)
A	1D	Shd*	Main	1	$30-$35	($10)
B	1D	Shd*	Main	2	$30-$35	($10)
C	2T	Shd*	Main	2	$30-$35	($10)

The only things I own which are still worth what they have cost me are my travel memories, the mind-pictures of places which I have been hoarding like a happy miser for more than half a century.

—Burton Holmes

The whole object of travel is not to set foot on foreign land; it is at last to set foot on one's own country as a foreign land.

—G.K. Chesterton

Washington
&
B.C., Canada

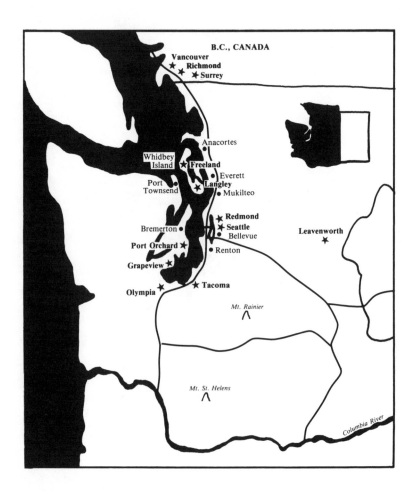

Washington wears two faces. On the west is a panorama of timbered mountains, deep canyons with rushing streams, fertile valleys, and shimmering, island-dotted bays. On the east lie black lava formations, the silver-green sagebrush plains, and rolling wheat country. The dividing line is the jagged, snowy crest of the majestic Cascade Range, which separates the mild, wet coastal climate from the drier east, where the mighty Columbia River carves a great arc, providing both water and power through its dam system.

Not far from the Interstate 5 mainline is Mount St. Helens, Washington's most famous performing mountain, which dominates the southern end of the Cascades. After losing thirteen hundred feet of its peak in the recent eruption, Mount St. Helens now stands at eighty-three hundred feet. Visitors to this national monument can learn a lot about volcanos from the daily interpretative programs. You can even call ahead for a volcanic activity report—just in case Mount St. Helens decides to blow again.

Further north, Washington's most famous mountain, glacier-mantled Mount Rainier, towers nearly three miles above sea level. A network of state and forest roads and three hundred miles of hiking trails provide access to this stately, pristine mountain. With thirty-four square miles of glaciers, it is the United States' largest single-peak glacier system outside of Alaska.

Travelers going north on Highway 101 will most likely be headed for the wild, wet, and wooded Olympic Peninsula. The Olympic Mountains rise seven thousand feet above the Pacific and overlook some of the last wilderness beaches in the country. The national park is comprised of nearly a million acres of untouched wilderness. Within it are six hundred miles of hiking trails that take you from icy crags to driftwood-strewn beaches. Clamming, crabbing, and fishing are all rewarding along the impressive coastline. Hurricane Ridge, almost a mile high, provides the most accessible view of the Olympic Range. This knife-edged mountain ridge explodes with color when the wildflowers bloom in the summer. The Sol Duc Hot Springs testify to the region's volcanic origins.

Yearly rainfall on the peninsula exceeds one hundred forty inches, promoting the growth of skyscraping trees and the only coniferous rain forest in the world. The centuries-old spruces and hemlocks seem to possess the wisdom of their years, giving this dim emerald forest cathedral a striking solemnity. The park contains the largest known specimens of Douglas fir, red cedar, western hemlock, and Alaskan cedar. Imaginative hikers might look for elves hiding beneath the immense ferns or dancing on the moss-carpeted forest floor.

Directly east is Puget Sound, a saltwater arm of the Pacific. Its hundreds of bays and inlets provide a total of no less than eighteen hundred miles of shoreline, much of it tree-lined and unspoiled. Getting around is sure to involve Washington's fleet of ferries, part of the state highway system.

The largest of Puget Sound's islands is Whidbey, approximately fifty miles long, where homes of the early settlers still dot the shore. Coupeville, one of the oldest towns in the state, has been restored and features Victorian buildings and picturesque shops. There are several parks on the island, including one of the state's finest at Deception Pass, where a bridge spans a gorge that is notorious for its unpredictable tidal currents.

From here it is a short distance to Mount Erie, about five miles south of Anacortes, where you can get a good view of Mounts Baker and Rainier, the Olympic Peninsula, the Cascades, and the San Juan Islands. A paved road ascends its thirteen hundred-foot summit.

A more intimate view of the San Juans can be had on a spectacular ferry ride, which leaves from Anacortes and weaves its way through this archipelago of one hundred seventy-two isles. The recreational opportunities in the San Juans are many—boating, water skiing, scuba diving, fishing, hiking, and bicycling.

Seattle, a city of hills and lakes, offers a number of attractions, including Pioneer Square, the Space Needle, the Pike Place Open-Air Market, and the waterfront. Southeast of Seattle, near Fall City, is Snoqualmie Falls, which plunge a hundred feet farther than those of Niagara. A trail leads into the canyon. An antique steam engine chugs along a seven-mile loop, enabling railroad buffs to visit the falls by train.

Further east, the Wenatchee National Forest stretches along the eastern slope of the Cascades. Leavenworth, near its eastern boundary, is modeled after a Bavarian village and offers art and music activities in the summer, skiing in the winter. Scenic Tumwater Canyon is about six miles to the west, while glacier-fed Lake Chelan lies to the east. Surrounded by the peaks of the Cascades, the lake's bottom drops to four hundred feet below sea level.

Lake Chelan National Recreation Area, noted for its beauty and recreational opportunities, marks the southern boundary of the North Cascades National Park, one of the wildest and most rugged sections of the United States. There are three hundred living glaciers in the park. Largely a backcountry wilderness area, the hardy will encounter breathtaking scenery and wildlife. The North Cascade Highway, which links the Puget Sound area to the North Cascades, offers some of the most astonishing vistas of mountains and alpine meadows anywhere. (The eastern section of the highway is closed in winter.)

If you're looking for unspoiled beauty, you are sure to find it in Washington. Here sea, mountain, and desert converge to provide enough natural diversity to satisfy the most restless of spirits.

Llewop Bed & Breakfast   **(206) 275-2287**
Box 97, Grapeview, WA 98546
(Southwest Puget Sound, off Highway 3)

This huge contemporary home rests on a wooded knoll overlooking an orchard, Case Inlet, and Stretch Island, with the summit of Mount Rainier showing on clear days. It is endowed with many windows, skylights, and decks, so it's easy to feel at one with the incredible beauty of the environment. There are two bedrooms for guests, both as lovely as can be. Room A has a spacious private deck with full view. Hospitality at Llewop B&B might include a home-cooked dinner featuring oysters and clams from the beach and produce from the garden. Guests are welcome to sit around the living room fireplace, explore the property, swim, play pickleball, or unwind in the whirlpool spa (tub in bathroom on main floor). Most of all, Llewop is a place for restoration and relaxation. The Powell family wants you to enjoy their home as much as they enjoy sharing it.

No pets; families welcome; smoking on decks; full breakfast; TV; extra beds; enclosed swimming pool (heated in season); bathtub spa; pickleball court; canoes; golf course and restaurants four miles away; home-cooked dinner by reservation; airport pickup (Port Orchard). Clergy discount.

Room	Bed	Bath	Entrance	Floor	Daily Rates S - D	(EP)
A	1D	Pvt	Main	2	$30-$35	($10)
B	2T	Pvt	Main	1	$30-$35	($10)

Brown's Farm, A Bed & Breakfast Home Place   **(509) 548-7863**
11150 Highway 209, Leavenworth, WA 98826
(One and one-half miles north of town on road to Plain)

Leavenworth is a picturesque Bavarian village that overlooks the Wenatchee River and is outlined by snowcapped Icicle Ridge. Each season brings a celebration and thousands of visitors who are touched by the welcoming spirit that abides here. In the Chumstick Valley, you'll find Brown's Farm, A Bed & Breakfast Home Place. Steve and Wendi Brown, their three children, and the resident animals make staying at this large, country farmhouse a rare experience in homespun hospitality. The family worked together to build the house. It has exposed log beams, walls of local timber, a huge fireplace of stones from the Icicle Valley, multi-paned windows, and stained-glass accents created by Steve and Wendi. Two bedrooms and a bath on the main floor make wonderfully cozy guest quarters. The simplicity of the decor is refreshing. Nothing about the ambiance is contrived; the charm is all natural. I can't imagine a healthier atmosphere for children growing up—or anyone else, for that matter.

Dogs, cats, horses, chickens, and rabbits on premises; families welcome (crib for children under five at no charge; other children with sleeping bags at $5 each); no smoking in bedrooms; full country breakfast; sink in Room A; some cross-country skis and snowshoes available; hiking, swimming, rafting, and sleigh rides nearby. Brochure available.

Room	Bed	Bath	Entrance	Floor	Daily Rates S - D	(EP)
A	1T & 1Q	Shd*	Main	1	$60	($10)
B	1Q	Shd*	Main	1	$55	($10)

Pickerings' Landing
7825 Urquhart Street NW, Olympia, WA 98502
(Just outside Olympia, in lower Puget Sound)

(206) 866-4537
(Keep trying!!)

After driving along unhurried, woodsy back roads, arriving at Pickerings' Landing is like finding the treasure at rainbow's end. The pristine white house is set in a commanding position with a view straight up Dana Passage. The home and landscaped grounds are a vision of stunning beauty. The front yard slopes down to a beach where you can dig for clams, hunt for agates and shells, and observe a variety of shorebirds. The home is extremely comfortable, with three lovely guest rooms and many windows to allow sweeping vistas of waterways and Mount Rainier. Jo and Chris Pickering feel that they have "something too good not to share," and I certainly agree. If you plan a visit to Pickerings' Landing, be sure to allow enough time to explore the area, enjoy the home and its surroundings, and get to know your genial hosts.

Cat in residence; no pets; children over ten welcome; limited smoking; full breakfast; TV; AC; laundry privileges; boating; other meals (from the garden's bounty) by arrangement; Pacific Ocean is one hour west; Mount St. Helens National Park, one hour south; Seattle, an hour and a half north; airport pickup (Olympia, Sea-Tac).

Room	Bed	Bath	Entrance	Floor	Daily Rates S - D (EP)
A	1D	Shd*	Main	1	$35-$40
B	2T	Shd*	Main	1	$35-$40
C	1D	Shd*	Main	LL	$35-$40

Unicorn's Rest   **(206) 754-9613**
316 East Tenth Avenue, Olympia, WA 98501
(Six blocks from state Capitol)

Unicorn's Rest is an endearing little 1937 Cape Cod home on the edge of downtown Olympia. It is within safe walking distance of good restaurants, the state Capitol, and the new performing arts center. Two spacious dormer bedrooms are decorated with antiques and loving care. Each makes a cozy, comforting place where the busy traveler can pause for a good rest. Rooms have their own sinks and a convenient shared bath. During your stay, the house is yours to use as your own—for visiting with friends, an informal business meeting, or just taking it easy. A host (Hal, Rita, or Rozanne) is always on hand to tell you of Olympia and the Puget Sound area or to assist you with arrangements. Their aim is to make Unicorn's Rest for every guest a favored spot, one to return to again and again.

No pets; no smoking in bedrooms; older children only; full breakfast; deck. Brochure available.

Room	Bed	Bath	Entrance	Floor	Daily Rates S - D	(EP)
A	1Q	Shd*	Main	2	$29-$39	($10)
B	1K	Shd*	Main	2	$33-$43	($10)

Ogle's Bed & Breakfast   **(206) 876-9170**
1307 Dogwood Hill SW, Port Orchard, WA 98366
(Overlooking Sinclair Inlet)

Picturesque Port Orchard Marina has a deep harbor and easy access to picnic areas, markets, historical sites, and the quaint town of Port Orchard. It has long been a favorite of Puget Sound seafarers. Whether you arrive by land or by sea, Ogle's B&B is a lovely place to drop anchor and let yourself be pampered by the gracious hospitality of Quentin and Louise Ogle. They seem to have anticipated a traveler's every need with an array of thoughtful amenities. The main guest room is very attractive, spacious, and comfortable. A smaller guest room with a jaunty, nautical theme is located just off the large den where Louise makes the wool braided rugs that enliven the decor. The home's hillside location affords indoor or outdoor breakfast dining with a view. The Olympic Mountains are sometimes visible, and the peninsula waits to be explored. Take a quick, walk-on ferry ride to Bremerton or a leisurely hour's trip through Puget Sound to Seattle. At Ogle's B&B, you can count on shipshape accommodations and a breakfast that will delight the gourmet.

Friendly Maine Coon Tabby cat in residence; no pets; children over twelve welcome; smoking in common areas only; full breakfast; TV; VCR; large library; music listening area; public transportation includes Airporter service between Sea-Tac and Port Orchard. $20 rate for Room B if traveling as third person.

Room	Bed	Bath	Entrance	Floor	Daily Rates S - D	(EP)
A	1Q	Shd	Main	1G	$30-$35	
B	1T	½ Pvt	Main	1G	$25	

207

Cedarym, A Colonial Bed & Breakfast   **(206) 868-4159**
1011 240th Avenue NE, Redmond, WA 98053
(Twenty-five minutes from Seattle; East Sammamish Plateau)

It's a rarity on the West Coast to walk into a home and feel that you've stepped back in time, not one, but *two* centuries. Creating an authentic Colonial-style home was a labor of love for Mary Ellen and Walt Brown. They have left out no detail—wide plank pine floors, wrought iron lift latches, stenciled walls, bullseye glass over the front door, hand-dipped candles—the list goes on and on. Guest quarters include two spacious bedrooms, each with an antique brass bed and a theme carried out by the stencil design, the Tulip and the Anchor. The exquisitely landscaped, cedar-encircled grounds add another dimension to a visit to Cedarym. There's a cottage garden of flowers and herbs, meditation paths to stroll, a large rose garden of both old and new varieties, and an irresistible gazebo-enclosed spa. A generous breakfast is served by the dining room fireplace each morning. A slice of Colonial America awaits you at Cedarym. Try not to miss it!

No pets; smoking outside only; full breakfast; TV in each room; gazebo spa; Model T car for sightseeing jaunts; Gilman Village (Issaquah), antique malls, Carnation and Remlinger Farms, Snoqualmie Falls, and beautiful country drives nearby; airport pickup (Sea-Tac). Excellent for small garden weddings.

Room	Bed	Bath	Entrance	Floor	Daily Rates S - D	(EP)
A	1D	Shd*	Main	2	$30-$40	($10)
B	1D	Shd*	Main	2	$30-$40	($10)

Galer Place (206) 282-5339
318 West Galer Street, Seattle, WA 98119
(South slope of Queen Anne Hill)

Galer Place has a British flavor that begins when you meet its owner. Chris Chamberlain is originally from England and ran a B&B in Sussex before moving to this country. She combines the best of that tradition with West Coast touches—a hot tub, relaxing informality, and freshly ground coffee with breakfast. Built in 1906 as a fine in-town family residence, Galer Place is now a warm and inviting guest house in a most convenient location. Antiques of the period and other special features create a unique mood in each of four bedrooms: the Brass, the Oak, the Mahogany, and the Rattan. The first floor parlor and dining room are natural places for guests to share that afternoon cuppa tea or the wonderful Continental breakfasts that Chris prepares. Galer Place will not only charm you, it will put many of Seattle's highlights right at your doorstep.

Dog in residence; no large pets; older children negotiable; garden hot tub; walking distance to Seattle Center; short bus ride to downtown Seattle; airport connections. Room B has a small deck; D has a private loft sitting room. Brochure available. 10% discount for five to seven days and midweek October-April; 15% discount for more than seven days.

Room	Bed	Bath	Entrance	Floor	Daily Rates S - D	(EP)
A	1D	Pvt	Main	2	$44-$49	($8)
B	1D	½ Pvt	Main	2	$41-$46	($8)
C	1D	Shd	Main	2	$35-$40	($8)
D	1Q	Shd	Main	2	$41-$46	($8)

Mercer Island Hideaway   **(206) 232-1092**
8820 SE 63rd Street, Mercer Island, WA 98040
(Three miles south of I-90, off Island Crest Way)

It's only a fifteen-minute drive east from Seattle, but when you cross the bridge over Lake Washington to Mercer Island, it seems like another world. The Williams' home, Mercer Island Hideaway, is a place of quiet luxury tucked into the lush green landscape. No matter which of the attractive accommodations you stay in, it will be like "sleeping in a forest," as one guest put it. The home has been beautifully renovated throughout and is kept in immaculate condition. Anyone with an interest in music will be at home here. The spacious living room has tall windows and a cathedral ceiling. It holds two grand pianos, a reed organ, and a harpsichord, any of which Mary Williams will play on request. She and Bill excel at making every guest feel special. Their personal warmth enhances the outstanding hospitality at Mercer Island Hideaway.

No pets; children welcome (family celebrations a specialty); smoking outside only; full breakfast; TV; crib and extra long beds available; ten-minute drive to Bellevue. Private baths usually available; Room C is a suite with patio entrance, fireplace, and wheelchair access.

Room	Bed	Bath	Entrance	Floor	Daily Rates S - D	(EP)
A	1Q	Shd*	Main	1	$30-$45	
B	1K	Shd*	Main	1	$30-$45	
C	2T & 1K	Shd*	Sep	1G	$45	($15)
D	1T	Shd*	Main	1G	$30	

Marit Nelson   **(206) 782-7900**
6208 Palatine Avenue N, Seattle, WA 98103
(Woodland Park area)

This cozy brick home is in a quiet north Seattle neighborhood with good access to freeways and public transportation. Here Marit Nelson offers her special version of Scandinavian hospitality. There's a very homey atmosphere, the kind that makes you feel like settling in for a while. A whimsical note is struck by the collection of stuffed bears flanking the stairs that lead to the guest rooms. Care has been taken to make each room comfy and attractive. Single travelers will be delighted with the view of water, mountains, and sunsets from Room B. A variety of guidebooks to Seattle and environs ensures that you'll find plenty to do, rain or shine. Breakfasts are delicious and beautifully served, a savory beginning to any day.

No pets, smoking, or RV parking; full breakfast; walking distance to Woodland Park Zoo; Norwegian spoken. Brochure available. Discount to AARP members.

Room	Bed	Bath	Entrance	Floor	Daily Rates S - D	(EP)
A	1Q	Shd	Main	2	$30-$35	
B	1T	Shd	Main	2	$25	

Pension Europa **(206) 328-1945**
1645 21st Avenue E, Seattle, WA 98112
(North Capitol Hill)

Pension Europa is suitably named. Liliane Gilbert is from Germany, has lived all over Europe, and has traveled extensively. The flavor of her home is decidedly old-world, full of grace and character. The upper floor accommodates guests in three bedrooms with a large shared bath. Rooms A and B have a partial view of the Cascades. The downstairs living room with fireplace has a warm, civilized atmosphere. Liliane prepares excellent breakfasts to suit her guests. She can suggest good routes for exploring the scenic wooded neighborhood on foot and recommend favorite spots nearby. Among the choices are the University of Washington Arboretum, Interlaken Park, Volunteer Park and Seattle Art Museum, or the exciting scene on Broadway. Pension Europa is convenient to downtown and the University of Washington, but its peaceful beauty makes it seem worlds away.

Small dog and cats in residence; full breakfast if desired; TV, radio, and down comforter in each room; kitchen privileges by arrangement; parks, tennis courts, jogging and bicycle trails nearby; good public transportation and airport connections; personal tours by arrangement; German and French spoken. Two-night minimum stay on holiday weekends; ask about discounts for extended stays.

Room	Bed	Bath	Entrance	Floor	Daily Rates S - D	(EP)
A	1D	Shd*	Main	2	$30-$35	($15)
B	1K	Shd*	Main	2	$35-$40	($15)
C	1D	Shd*	Main	2	$30-$35	

Keenan House (206) 752-0702
2610 North Warner, Tacoma, WA 98407
(Near University of Puget Sound)

If houses could smile, Keenan House would be grinning. The large marine-blue home has a friendly, welcoming look that doesn't deceive. Set on one of Tacoma's most pleasant old residential streets, it has matured gracefully and is tended with loving care by Mrs. Lenore Keenan. She offers British-style B&B much as she experienced on her travels through England. Accommodations are exceptionally clean and attractive. Soft-colored fabrics and wallcoverings, rich carpeting, and lovely furnishings appoint the three bedrooms on the second floor; a cozy attic suite occupies the third. Guests may spend leisure time downstairs in the comfortable living room or around the piano in the foyer. Mrs. Keenan serves full English breakfasts enhanced by some of her own house specialties. In fact, she manages to make everything at Keenan House special.

No pets; smoking on porch or balcony; good public transportation and airport connections; some French and Spanish spoken. Two full and two half-baths available. Rooms A and B share a balcony. Waterfront restaurants in Old Town, one mile away. Convenient to Point Defiance Park with new zoo and the Vashon Island Ferry. Double room with private bath available at $45.

Room	Bed	Bath	Entrance	Floor	Daily Rates S - D	(EP)
A	1Q	Shd*	Main	2	$35-$40	
B	1D	Shd*	Main	2	$35-$40	
C	2T	Shd*	Main	2	$35-$40	
D	3T	Shd*	Main	3	$35-$40	($15)

Pillars By The Sea

(206) 221-7738

1367 East Bayview Avenue, Freeland, WA 98249
(Eleven miles north of Mukilteo Ferry, right at Book Bay Bookstore)

The neat yellow home of Walker and Ellen Jordan has white pillars, white trim, and pure turn-of-the-century charm. Geraniums in window boxes and pretty stained-glass panels flanking the front door add lively splashes of color. Towering shade trees and a back yard that slopes down to historic Holmes Harbor complete the picture. The 1907 home has been restored to mint condition inside and out. Two handsomely appointed guest rooms with private baths occupy the upper floor. Room A has a view of the water, and B features down comforters and pillows. A larger, beautifully decorated guest room (C) and bath are on the main floor. Outstanding breakfasts are elegantly served with the harbor in sight. Walk to beaches or nearby Freeland Park, or visit the quaint seaside towns of Langley and Coupeville. But what you're most likely to remember about your visit are the serene beauty and unfailing graciousness at Pillars By The Sea.

No pets or smoking; full breakfast; porch and deck; horseback riding and bicycle rentals nearby; airport pickup (Oak Harbor). Brochure available. Weekly rate is $295; clergy discount.

Room	Bed	Bath	Entrance	Floor	Daily Rates S - D (EP)
A	1Q	Pvt	Sep	2	$55-$60
B	1Q	Pvt	Sep	2	$55-$60
C	1Q	Pvt	Main	1	$55-$60

The Orchard Bed & Breakfast　　　　　　　　　**(206) 221-7880**
619 Third Street, Langley, WA 98260
(South Whidbey Island)

　　Imagine a vintage farmhouse, with a large, wrap-around porch and a hanging swing, standing in the midst of an old orchard. It has been remodeled to perfection according to host Martha Murphy's vision of "a warm, family place where everyone can feel at home." The Orchard has a wholesome quality that reminds me of fresh apples and home-baked bread. Bountiful country breakfasts are served in the solarium adjacent to the kitchen. Two upstairs bedrooms are as pretty as they are comfortable. People who live in or visit South Whidbey appreciate the simple pleasures of a slow-paced life. There are forests to roam, berries to pick, and beaches to comb. Puget Sound is at your feet, and the Cascades loom in the background. You might enjoy reading a book in the front porch swing, or helping yourself to fruits and nuts on the trees in the yard. Everything about The Orchard inspires relaxation and doing as you please.

　　Children welcome; smoking outside only; full breakfast; TV; kitchen privileges; piano; cradle; toys and games; babysitters available; horseback trail rides nearby. Room A has a covered balcony. Brochure available. Weekly rates; special $70 rate for family of four in two rooms; no charge for small child in room with parent(s).

Room	Bed	Bath	Entrance	Floor	Daily Rates S - D	(EP)
A	1Q	Shd*	Main	2	$35-$45	
B	1D	Shd*	Main	2	$35-$45	

Sheila's Bed & Breakfast   **(604) 274-9179**
5860 Granville Avenue, Richmond, B.C. V7C 1E9
(Near Vancouver International Airport)

Many people find Sheila Ingram's home to be very well located. It's near enough to the airport to be handy, but not near enough to get the noise. A convenient trip by bus or car takes you north to downtown Vancouver and to most of the places you'll want to visit. The contemporary home is attractively furnished, spacious, and immaculate inside. It has a rambling floor plan that makes bedrooms seem separate and private. Sheila encourages guests to enjoy the entire house as they wish. The pretty, landscaped back yard is used for breakfast alfresco, a treat on sunny days, but Sheila's home is a comforting place to be, regardless of the weather.

No pets; children welcome; no smoking in bedrooms; full breakfast; extra beds available; public transportation; airport pickup by arrangement.

Room	Bed	Bath	Entrance	Floor	Daily Rates S - D	(EP)
A	2T	Pvt	Main	1	$30-$50	($10)
B	2T	Shd	Main	1	$25-$40	($10)

Rates stated in Canadian funds.

The Hirsch's Place   **(604) 588-3326**
10336-145 A Street, Surrey, B.C. V3R 3S1
(Twenty-five minutes east of downtown Vancouver)

It's an easy commute to Vancouver by freeway from The Hirsch's Place. The suburban location has the feel of being in the country, yet all the conveniences you could want are close by. For extended stays or travelers who'd like more privacy, a yard, and ample living space, this comfortable blue duplex couldn't be better. The side used for guests has a living room, dining room, full kitchen, two bedrooms, and a bath. The large fenced yard has a fish pool, hothouse, and garden. Hosts Barb and Andy Hirsch are on hand to visit or to lend any assistance you might need, but the privacy of guests is always respected. With so much to recommend it, The Hirsch's Place could just be *your* kind of place.

Children and small house dogs welcome; no smoking in bedrooms; TV; kitchen; laundry service, babysitting, playpen and high chair available; good public transportation. One bedroom has king-sized waterbed. Brochure available. 10% discount for seven days or longer.

Room	Bed	Bath	Entrance	Floor	Daily Rates S - D	(EP)
A	D	Shd*	Sep	1	$40-$45	($10)
B	K	Shd*	Sep	1	$40-$45	($10)

Rates stated in Canadian funds.

217

Creekside Bed & Breakfast   **(604) 734-3369**
1124 Ironwork Passage, False Creek, Vancouver, B.C. V6H 3P1
(On waterfront looking north to Vancouver city, across from Expo site)

Vancouver's False Creek community is a choice address for residents and visitors alike. It's a contemporary car-less neighborhood with an old-world flavor and an air of exciting diversity. Beryl Wilson, host of Creekside B&B, is active in the community; she's founder and editor of its newspaper, *The Creek*. Her home faces the waterfront where there's an endless parade of salty sloops, seagulls, joggers, and friendly folk out for a stroll. You can keep your eye on the action from the breakfast table, then set out on foot to explore the area for yourself. A view of mountains, the skyline of Vancouver, Granville Island, and the 1986 Expo site is your constant companion. When you're ready for a break, relax in a garden setting on the brick patio that faces the courtyard in back. It's easy to make yourself at home at Creekside B&B, a true urban oasis.

Small pet by arrangement; no space for children; no smoking preferred; public transportation. Creekside is located across the courtyard from Spruce Haus.

Room	Bed	Bath	Entrance	Floor	Daily Rates S - D	(EP)
A	1Q	Pvt	Main	1	$35-$55	

Rates stated in Canadian funds.

Spruce Haus   **(604) 738-8589**
1183 Forge Walk, False Creek, Vancouver, B.C. V6H 3R1
(On waterfront looking north to Vancouver city, across from Expo site)

The waterfront False Creek redevelopment has become quite the place to be in Vancouver, and I can understand why. From Lois Meyerhoff's three-story townhouse you have a view of water, city, and mountains. Picturesque marinas dot the sea wall just steps from the front door. It's an easy walk to Granville Island's Public Market, choice restaurants, playhouses, and interesting crafts shops. A quick walk-on ferry ride and you can be on Vancouver's downtown side or in Stanley Park. Lois is a patio gardener and her entire home, inside and out, is bedecked with greenery and blooms. Guests may choose between a room with twin beds and one with a king-sized bed and a view. You might enjoy picking up some food and wine from the market and creating your own supper to enjoy on one of the decks. The easygoing atmosphere and friendly hospitality at Spruce Haus will make you feel like a native in no time at all.

Cable TV in each room; sundecks; public transportation; sailboat (charters available), canoe, bicycles, laundry and kitchen facilities available. Brochure available. Rates will be $10 higher during Expo '86 (May 1-October 15).

Room	Bed	Bath	Entrance	Floor	Daily Rates S - D	(EP)
A	2T	Shd*	Main	2	$45-$55	
B	1K	Shd*	Main	2	$45-$55	

Rates stated in Canadian funds.

219

CALIFORNIA

OREGON

CALIFORNIA

OREGON

WASHINGTON

B.C., CANADA

ORDERING ADDITIONAL ITEMS

Please send me the following items: (I enclose payment where appropriate.)

☐ _____ additional copies of *BED & BREAKFAST HOMES DIRECTORY* (4th edition) at $8.95 each plus $1 postage and handling for first copy, 50¢ for each additional copy to same address

☐ A one-year subscription to *The Knighttime Companion* at $10 per year (6 issues)

☐ A sample copy of *The Knighttime Companion* at $2

☐ Annotated list of other publications that we offer, known as *The Knighttime Collection* (free)

Name _____

Address _____

City/State/Zip _____

Send as a gift to: (Use extra paper for additional gifts.)

Name _____

Address _____

City/State/Zip _____

Gift card should read: _____

KNIGHTTIME PUBLICATIONS, P.O. Box 591, Cupertino, CA 95015

CUT HERE

APPLICATION TO BECOME A B&B HOST

Name(s) _____

Mailing address _____

City/State/Zip _____

Telephone _____

Best time to phone you _____

Brief description of your home and room(s) available:

_____

_____

_____

_____

_____

_____

_____

_____

_____

_____

There is a two-year listing fee which is equal to two times the highest (double) rate you charge for one night's lodging. (Example: If your rate is $45, listing fee is $90.) Hosts must maintain clean, comfortable accommodations and a hospitable manner toward guests.

Signature _____

Date _____

From: _____

_____

_____

Diane Knight
Knighttime Publications
P.O. Box 591
Cupertino, CA 95015

CUT HERE

---------------------FOLD HERE ---------------------

STAPLE OR TAPE

B&B TRAVELER'S REPORT

Knighttime Publications would like to receive any comments you may have about your experiences while using this directory. Please report any comment, suggestion, compliment or criticism as indicated:

Name and location of host home _____

_____

Date of visit_____Length of stay_____

Comments _____

_____

_____

_____

_____

_____

_____

_____

_____

_____

_____

Your name _____

Address _____

City/State/Zip _____

Telephone _____

CUT HERE

From: _____

_____

_____

Diane Knight
Knighttime Publications
P.O. Box 591
Cupertino, CA 95015

— — — — — — — — — — — — — FOLD HERE — — — — — — — — — — —

CUT HERE

STAPLE OR TAPE

B&B TRAVELER'S REPORT

Knighttime Publications would like to receive any comments you may have about your experiences while using this directory. Please report any comment, suggestion, compliment or criticism as indicated:

Name and location of host home _____

_____

Date of visit_____Length of stay_____

Comments _____

_____

_____

_____

_____

_____

_____

_____

_____

_____

_____

Your name _____

Address _____

City/State/Zip _____

Telephone _____

CUT HERE

From: _____

Diane Knight
Knighttime Publications
P.O. Box 591
Cupertino, CA 95015

— — — — — — — — — — — — FOLD HERE — — — — — — — — — — —

CUT HERE

STAPLE OR TAPE

B&B Home Locations

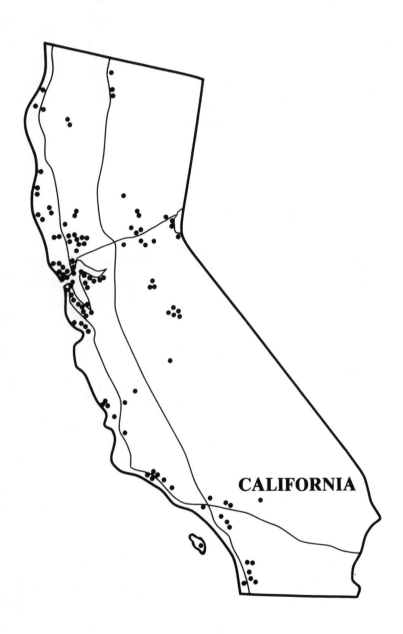

CALIFORNIA